Imperial Subjects

Imperial Subjects

Citizenship in an age of crisis and empire

COLIN MOOERS

B L O O M S B U R Y

NEW YORK • LONDON • NEW DELHI • SYDNEY

Bloomsbury Academic

An imprint of Bloomsbury Publishing Inc

1385 Broadway	50 Bedford Square
New York	London
NY 10018	WC1B 3DP
USA	UK

www.bloomsbury.com

Bloomsbury is a registered trade mark of Bloomsbury Publishing Plc

First published 2014

© Colin Mooers, 2014

Library of Congress Cataloging-in-Publication Data
A catalog record for this book is available from the Library of Congress.

ISBN: HB: 978-1-4411-5249-7
PB: 978-1-4411-9251-6
ePub: 978-1-4411-6493-3
ePDF: 978-1-4411-3514-8

Typeset by Integra Software Services Pvt. Ltd.
Printed and bound in the United States of America

Contents

Acknowledgements

Works of this sort are always collective endeavours. The ideas and arguments developed here are the result of countless discussions with friends, colleagues and comrades over many years. I thank especially David McNally and Alan Sears for their careful reading of the manuscript at various stages in its development. Their suggestions and criticisms have, I am sure, saved me from making many more errors than may be evident in the final text. Thanks also to the anonymous reviewer of an earlier draft of the manuscript and to the editorial staff at Bloomsbury for their invaluable suggestions. Whatever faults remain are my own. *Un gran abrazo* to the renowned Chilean artist Alfredo Jaar, for providing the photo and cover design. Thanks also to Atif Nasim, whose research and editorial skills were indispensable throughout the completion of the manuscript. Final thanks must go to Marnie Fleming, who tolerated my wilder flights of abstraction with equanimity, understanding and love. This book is dedicated to her.

Introduction: Capitalism, Citizenship and Empire

The title of this book may strike some readers as quaintly anachronistic. To speak of 'imperial subjects', it might be thought, is to conjure a faded past of jodhpurs, pith helmets and Kipling by candlelight. Equally vexing might be the conjunction of the term 'citizenship' with 'capitalism' and 'imperialism'. To such readers, the suggestion that there might be some necessary, as opposed to accidental, set of forces or processes which link these three terms will seem tendentious. But the burden of my argument is to show precisely that the coincidence of these economic and political forms is not accidental. Indeed, both forms of rule have their origins in the replacement of 'extra-economic' forms of civic status which existed in pre-capitalist societies with the predominantly market-based forms that emerged with early capitalism. And, while it is certainly true that there are vast differences between the formal empires of the eighteenth and nineteenth centuries and the largely informal, market-based type of imperial rule which exists today, our 'colonial present', as Derek Gregory asserts, still bears strong continuities with the past.

The British colonial empire of the second half of the nineteenth century was constructed on the basis of the capitalist ideology of free trade and private property, though it was careful to choke off any such practices among its colonies. India, for example, was arguably more economically and socially underdeveloped at independence in 1947 than it had been in the eighteenth century. To be an 'imperial subject' in nineteenth- and early twentieth-century India meant the continuation of a form of legal servitude backed by force and fealty to the British crown. For the white-settler colonialists in Canada or Australia, the terms of colonial subject-hood were far less burdensome, which is more than can be said for the indigenous peoples they displaced. The violent dispossession and enslavement of the indigenous peoples of the Americas was an essential precondition of all later forms of the capitalist development. For many indigenous communities, numerous forms of colonial servitude still remain, while the most basic aspects of citizenship, like the right to vote, have only been grudgingly granted in the second half of the twentieth century. The effects of internal colonialism kept them marginalized from market relations. More recently, however, the predations of 'extractive capitalism' in the form of resource development have subjected their communities to violent forms of market dispossession with very little promise of long-term employment in the wage-economy. But, even for the white-settler colonists an elaborate, racialized class hierarchy was key to their civic status. Irish indentured labourers in the American South, for example, were considered sufficiently non-white to be tried out first as chattel slaves by the great plantation owners before they turned to African slaves as a source of cheap and dependable labour. For those who were the subjects of colonization, in other words, different forms of legal servitude were allowed to coexist with civic forms more appropriate to capitalism well into the twentieth century. By the same reasoning, Marx referred to plantation slavery in the American South as 'capitalist slavery' because of the way in which cotton production was inserted within a world market dominated by the British cotton industry. In the technical terminology Marx would use in *Capital*, these forms of legal servitude represented the 'formal subsumption of labour' to capital. That is, while their outward form appeared to be still pre-capitalist, these labour forms had already been incorporated into the logic of capitalism. The same principle may be said to hold for the relationship between territorial empire and informal empire; in specific historical conditions, both forms may be present at the same time and in the same location. The people of Palestine, for example, can be said to experience both a version of formal settler-colonialism by the Israeli state, alongside, and often in direct cooperation with, larger and more informal regional and global imperial powers. The mutually reinforcing link between these two forms of empire can be seen in the way in which Palestinian labour functions both as a reserve army of cheap labour under the direct military control of the Israeli state and, more informally, as a source of migrant labour in the greater Gulf region.

What makes these examples of settler-colonialism different from the older colonial empires is that they are inserted within a global system which is today unequivocally capitalist. Following the First World War, it became evident that the maintenance of territorial empire was actually a hindrance in the competition for hegemony in the world market, and in the face of nascent anti-colonial struggles, most states opted to dispense with their colonial holdings following the Second World War. Imperial power thereafter would rest chiefly on non-territorial, market-based forms of domination and control. What is important to note here is that, over time, a new definition of imperialism was emerging, one in which older forms of colonial surplus-extraction based on direct political and military coercion were being replaced with more indirect, market-based forms of exploitation in which what mattered was the production of capitalist profit. Forms of internal colonialism would persist but in ways adapted to the domination of capitalist market relations.

Capitalist social-property relations first emerged in English agriculture in the seventeenth and eighteenth centuries. There, agrarian capitalism had developed through domestic colonization, the removal of 'waste' and the application of agricultural 'improvements', and the enclosure of common lands and a new conception of property rights (Mooers 1991; Wood 2003). The consolidation of agrarian capitalism through enclosure, expropriation and the destruction of customary rights was never a peaceful affair; the 'primitive accumulation of capital', as Marx (1977, 875) recognized, 'is written in the annals of mankind in letters of blood and fire'. These early transformations wrought by primitive accumulation had several key consequences: first, a new class of producers came into being that was now wholly dependent on the market for survival – the modern class of wage-labour. Wage-labour would become the social precondition for the emergence of capitalist industry as well as for the particular form taken by citizenship rights and democracy in liberal capitalist societies. In terms of empire, the advent of agrarian capitalism opened up new possibilities for colonization as well as providing a reliable social safety-valve for those who had been dispossessed by land enclosures in the metropoles by providing them with new opportunities as colonial settlers. Moreover, its colonies were able to provide it with the necessary inputs (often extracted through the use of slave labour) to fuel capitalist industry at home (Wood 2002, 83–88).

Thus, capitalism and imperialism were from the beginning conjoined. Most importantly, they both depended on a new type of social subject: one without direct access to means of subsistence and therefore wholly dependent on the market for survival. Market coercion, which relies on the indirect and impersonal forces of the market – the choice between working and starving as Marx would put it, – was becoming the dominant form of social control and surplus extraction. In the most developed capitalist regions, market identities were gradually replacing older pre-capitalist forms of social ascription based on hierarchies of birth and legal status. Moreover, capitalist social-property relations were uniquely compatible with ideologies of civic freedom and equality embodied in modern forms of citizenship (Wood 2006). For those who were forced to sell their labour in order to survive, the rights and freedoms of labour were double-edged. While capitalist rights and freedoms represented a real advance over all pre-capitalist forms, they were also strictly limited to the political sphere so as not to interfere with the more fundamental rights and freedoms of capitalist economic interests and private property. In effect, the political powers rooted in the productive sphere had been devolved to owners of private property; in the economic realm, private interests reigned supreme. The application of direct coercion now rested with the state, the primary purpose of which was the enforcement and protection of rights of property.

The liberal subject of modern capitalist citizenship, which emerged in the most developed capitalist societies, was shaped by the separation between economics and politics made possible by primitive accumulation. And although the actual form of this separation has varied widely depending on the historical configuration of class forces in different societies, in its 'classic form' this separation has been key to the coexistence of civic equality alongside class inequality. As Ellen Wood has observed:

> In capitalist society, primary producers are subject to economic compulsions which are independent of their political status. The power of the capitalist to appropriate the surplus labour of workers is not dependent on a privileged juridical or civic status but on the workers' propertylessness, which obliges them to exchange their labour power for a wage in order to gain access to the means of labour and subsistence. Workers are subject both to the power of capital and to the imperatives of competition and profit maximization. The separation of civic status and class position in capitalist societies thus has two sides: on the one hand, the right of citizenship is not determined by socio-economic position – and in this sense, capitalism can co-exist with formal democracy – on the other hand, civic equality does not directly affect class inequality, and formal democracy leaves class exploitation fundamentally intact.
>
> (Wood 1995, 201)

The separation of the economic and political spheres thus places real constraints on what can be accomplished by the democratic exercise of citizenship rights in the political sphere alone. By placing questions of class exploitation and the appropriation of economic surpluses, so to speak, 'beyond the pale', it has often been a challenge for class-based movements to affect change in the fundamental structure of capitalist social relations – that is, unless they have been able to somehow bridge the divide between the political and economic realms. Indeed, many of the most fundamental achievements in citizenship rights over the past two centuries – from the right to vote for working class women and men to more recent gains in gender and sexual rights – have been won by movements prepared to challenge the boundary between these two spheres of social life. However, a fundamental paradox remains: despite important gains in civil and social rights often won through hard-fought battles against systemic oppression, such rights have always remained precarious and qualitatively subordinate to capitalist property rights. As the historian David Montgomery (1995, 2) observed of the nineteenth-century struggle of American workers for full citizenship rights, the 'more that active participation in government was opened to the propertyless strata of society, the less capacity elected officials seemed to have to shape the basic contours of social life'. The same point could be made about the condition of African Americans in the period since the civil rights movement of the 1960s or indeed of many other social movements which have realized gains in democratic rights only to see them diminished by the realities of class inequality and the encroachment of market power into every aspect of social life. This is not to suggest that formal democracy, civil rights and liberties and representative government are not an improvement on less democratic political forms. For those who have been denied basic civil rights historically, such as women, racialized groups, indigenous peoples or gays and lesbians, winning full citizenship rights is of great significance. But it is equally true that capitalism has had to limit the substance of these rights in ways which make them compatible with the rule of capital (Wood 1995, 252–253).

The largely non-territorial or informal nature of contemporary imperialism requires only that markets be open to foreign capital and that the rule of law exists to protect the property rights of investors and ostensibly free and contractual relations between buyers and sellers of labour. However, this is only half the story. As we shall see in later chapters, *force* remains indispensible both to the achievement of market 'openness' where it does not yet exist and to securing ongoing compliance with the rights of capital. The ideological justification for informal empire, and an article of faith for much of mainstream international relations, rests on the assumption that states interact in much the way that free and equal citizens interact. In other words, imperial domination of weaker states by more powerful ones is disguised by an appearance of equality in the same way that formal democracy disguises class inequality. As Wood observes:

> There is an analogy here between citizens in a capitalist democracy and states in a global capitalist empire. The democratic polity is made up of formally free and equal civic individuals, just as the global order is made up of formally free and equal sovereign states. And just as citizenship tends to mask class domination in capitalism, legal state sovereignty tends to mask imperial domination.
>
> (Wood 2006, 15)

However, the internal relationship between informal empire and citizenship has never been static; indeed important differences exist between the 'Open

Door' imperialism practiced by the US for much of the twentieth century and more recent developments. Very few today hold to the expansive view of citizenship that dominated during the so-called 'golden era' of welfare-state capitalism following the Second World War. T.H. Marshall's well-known theory of citizenship rights posited an historical evolution from civil, to political to social rights, over the three centuries from the eighteenth to the twentieth century (Marshall 2009). At the time, this genial view was typical of an optimism shared by liberals and social democrats alike. The belief that sufficient funds could be gleaned from taxes on rising wages and profits to pay for the myriad social programmes which were being implemented in much of the developed capitalist world was of a piece with the Cold War imperialist ideology which prevailed at the time. To the natural rights individualism of classical liberalism was added a new toleration for the state. 'National individualism', as James O'Connor dubbed it, rested upon a widespread toleration of missiles and regional wars in the respective 'spheres of influence' of the two superpowers, so long as general social consumption was rising (O'Connor 1984).

The story since the return of capitalist crisis in the mid-1970s and the subsequent collapse of the Stalinist states at the beginning of the 1990s has seen the emergence of a form of neo-liberal capitalism which consciously roots itself in an earlier era of capitalism combined with a 'new imperialism' which looks both familiar and different than its Cold War predecessor. Neo-liberalism has, from the beginning, been 'about the restoration of class power' (Harvey 2007, 31). The now familiar mantra of deregulation of both industry and financial markets, assaults on the capacities of organized labour and the opening up of vast new areas of the planet to capital penetration are intimately linked to the dynamics of the 'new imperialism'. Indeed, what Harvey has aptly described as 'accumulation through dispossession' (Harvey 2003) is the defining feature of today's neo-liberal imperialism. With much of the cant of Cold War ideology, of 'freedom' versus 'totalitarian communism', now swept away, global capitalism has had to seek new ideological justifications more firmly rooted in its own processes and outcomes. And while neo-liberalism has provided a unifying ideology for capitalists and state managers bent on implementing its free market nostrums, it has had only grudging ideological appeal for the mass of the population. Outside the ranks of Tea Party populism in the US, the rise in social inequality, falling real wages, job insecurity and growing levels of indebtedness have not produced the kind of 'social cohesion' hoped for by its defenders. What it has attempted to (re) produce is a version of natural rights liberalism of a much older vintage, shorn of any expectation of state provision. Remaking 'the self a portfolio' (Martin 2007, 187) and keeping oneself in virtual circulation via the internet and social media have become imperatives of personal marketing in much of the developed capitalist world. Civic life has been remodelled on the vagaries of financial markets as risk and insecurity have become the primary motivators of individual action. A new ideology of what I have elsewhere called 'lean citizenship' (Mooers 2001, 72) has been fashioned, modelled on a 'flexible', 'mobile' and 'agile' workforce, ready to seize whatever opportunities market forces might throw in their path. Since September, 2001, the 'war on terror' has added a new calculus of fear and anxiety, sometimes deliberately, to the already simmering insecurities of everyday life under capitalism.

It is not by chance, therefore, that a new discourse of human rights has emerged in the era of neo-liberalism, not only as an internal critique of many of its excesses but also as an effective cover for the new imperialism as a form of 'humanitarian intervention'. The 'limited objectives of many rights discourses', Harvey (2007, 178) notes, 'makes it all too easy to absorb them within the neoliberal frame ... it has been all too easy to co-opt human rights issues as "swords of empire"' from Kosovo to Haiti and from Afghanistan and Iraq to Libya and Syria. Whatever else the recent wars of empire have been about, one of their chief aims has been to impose through *force* what has been only imperfectly realized through *consent* in the heartlands of capitalism.

Iraq has become a kind of laboratory of enforced neo-liberal experimentation in much the way that Chile had been in the 1970s. In 2004, the US appointed proconsul in Iraq, Paul Bremer, boasted: 'It's a full scale economic overhaul. We're going to create the first real free market economy in the Arab world' (quoted in Doran 2012, 9). Despite not getting everything it wanted out of Iraq, judged from the standpoint of securing the basic principles of corporate rule and obeisance to the international institutions which govern international capital, the US invasion has been a success. On the other hand, with 1.2 million deaths directly attributable to the invasion and another five million people displaced, judged from the standpoint the Iraqi people, it has been an abject and disgraceful failure: 'Violence and torture have been the hallmarks of the US in Iraq, not democracy and the rule of law' (Doran 2012, 239). 'Military neoliberalism', although it springs from the same imperatives in the capitalist accumulation process as other forms of market-based globalization, is distinctive in the role it plays in enforcing the differentiated structure of regional and national inequalities that define the global system and the appropriation and distribution of economic surpluses. Therefore, extra-economic violence, with whatever new clothes it may have adorned itself, remains an indispensable part of the imperial system.

There is, then, an important sense in which military and other types of neo-liberal dispossession form two sides of the same coin with regard to the form and content of citizenship in our own age of empire. Each side of the coin has fashioned its own particular mystifying ideology: military neo-liberalism has combined the velvet glove of 'humanitarian intervention' with the mailed fist of invasion and occupation, while neo-liberalism more generally has spawned a precarious citizen-subject whose identity is now defined by risk, uncertainty and an intensified commodification of the self. The long-term goal in both instances is the same: the creation of social and political subjects whose domain of democratic participation is circumscribed by the imperatives of capital accumulation and the market. In the heartlands of capitalism, 'the war on terror' has warranted a direct attack on the oldest and the most basic of liberal civic rights; freedoms of movement, speech, association, privacy, and, in some European states, religion, have been modified or curtailed in many countries with those most severely affected coming from so-called 'non-western' backgrounds. The molecular changes wrought by thirty years of neo-liberal policies have slowly but surely eaten away at the fabric of hard won 'social citizenship rights' to secure work, housing, healthcare and social security. Since 2008, the imposition of austerity across the capitalist world has greatly accelerated the displacement of social rights in favour of a new regime of social debt. In the Global South, the combination of military and market-based forms of neo-liberalism have meant that even the most basic legal rights of citizenship, where they have been achieved at all, remain precarious. In those regions such as Latin America, where Leftist governments have attempted to expand the domain of social rights within a regional economy still dominated by private capital, they have been harassed by coup attempts, electoral interference and economic sanctions.

To be an 'imperial subject' today, therefore, means very different things in different regions of the global system. Exposure to extra-economic violence as a means of imposing market dependence is much more the common experience in the Global South than in the North. As Robert Brenner (2006, 93–94) points out, 'the exercise of coercion rather than hegemony has been distributed not so much temporally, or according to who is President, but geographically – with hegemony fit for regions of advanced capitalism, domination appropriate for the poor countries of the planet'. How and through what means capitalist dispossession takes place varies, depending on where one is situated within the global system, pre-existing social conditions and, crucially, forms of resistance.[1] Some may think it odd that I use the term 'imperial subjects' to describe a global condition affecting populations in both the Global North and South. However, I use the term advisedly, not to soften the real differences noted earlier, but to highlight the fact that the rights and freedoms of citizens in the Global North have always been closely tied, through a kind of Faustian bargain, to the fortunes of empire. During the Cold War, the expansion of social security was inextricably tied to the expansion of America's global empire and the national security state. More recently, however, the terms of this 'bargain' have become severely strained. The 'new imperialism' which emerged since the end of the Cold War cannot make the same promises of national and social security. The 'war on terror' sustains itself not on the promise of a better life but rather on a political economy of fear of unseen 'others', attacks on legal and social rights and spiralling social inequality. Thus, for the vast majority, the material benefits of empire have become increasingly sparse; for those at the bottom, the conditions of everyday life have begun to converge with those in the Global South: falling real wages, deteriorating working conditions and longer hours of work and the downsizing and privatization of non-market public goods such as healthcare, education, pensions and the like. As living standards have fallen, household debt has risen alongside sovereign debt. As a consequence, individual and collective life has become more and more tied to the dictates of financial capital and the global institutions like the International Monetary Fund (IMF) and the World Bank which oversee its interests. A whole new repertoire of financial instruments has been developed for transferring wealth from the world's producers to those who own and control its substantial wealth. Accumulation through dispossession, although its impact is felt differentially within the imperial system, is nonetheless a global phenomenon since imperatives of capitalism have become increasingly universal.

Since 2008, the return of global capitalist crisis has disrupted the neat ideological fit between neo-liberalism, liberal citizenship and imperialism. Profound economic crises, Marx believed, have the effect of 'tearing away the metaphysical veil' which obscures the underlying social basis of capital accumulation. In such moments, the intricate superstructure of institutions which have arisen to buttress class rule may quickly begin to lose their legitimacy. The twenty-eight million jobs which have evaporated worldwide since 2008 have greatly affected the supremacy of the neo-liberal worldview. We have already seen how fragile faith in existing institutions can become in Europe and elsewhere as larger numbers of people, especially among the young, face the prospect of long-term joblessness and poverty. Rising unemployment combined with a perceived lack of fairness in the way in which the burden of the crisis has been shared has heightened levels of social and political struggle in many regions of the globe, including the heartlands of capitalism in Europe and North America. The International Labour Organization (ILO) reports in its first such attempt to measure social unrest, that in

> 40 percent of the 119 countries for which estimates could be performed, the risk of social unrest has increased significantly since 2010. Similarly, 58 percent of countries show an increase in the percentage of people who

report a worsening of standards of living. And confidence in the ability of national governments to address the situation has weakened in half the countries.

World of Work Report (2011, 2)

It is hardly surprising, therefore, that Occupy Wall Street and other anti-austerity movements, like those sparked by student struggles against neo-liberal education 'reform' in Chile and Quebec in 2011–2012 or those being played out in the streets of Greece and Spain, have been so effective in 'changing the conversation' about the causes and effects of the current crisis. Part of this conversation, the part which has infuriated many mainstream media and academic pundits, has been its multivocal character. Despite their uneven ebbs and flows, the surely remarkable thing about these movements has been their ability to absorb into their ranks a multiplicity of formerly quite isolated and sectional struggles – from labour and immigrant struggles to anti-racism, housing rights and anti-war struggles. What is important about such developments, in principle if not yet in practice, is the promise of breaching the divide between economics and politics so vital in sustaining the 'metaphysical veil' which obscures the true nature of capitalist social relations.

Theorizing citizenship

All of this suggests an urgent need for a holistic approach to theorizing contemporary citizenship; an unapologetic reassertion of the 'grand narratives' so derided in recent decades by a now exhausted 'postmodern turn'. As one observer put it, 'a global theory of citizenship remains one of the leading desiderata of contemporary social theory' (Beiner 1995, 115). The academic literature has cited a number of events which have altered traditional views on citizenship: the collapse of communism and resurgence of nationalism; globalization, warfare and migration; erosion of the welfare state in the industrialized world; new rights claims by women, gays and other minorities.[2] This catalogue of changes has prompted some theorists to claim that older liberal and republican models of citizenship are in the process of dissolution (Cohen 1999). Postmodern theorists have gone further to suggest that the entire modernist lexicon of universal rights, freedom and equality should be junked in favour of a democratic politics rooted in notions of identity and difference.[3]

Too often, however, this work has been highly circumscribed by what Frederic Jameson (1998, 96) has called 'the current four c's of the ideological re-equipment of late capitalism – contracts, constitutions, citizenship and civil society ... well-worn vagrants newly bathed, shaven, and dressed up in respectable new clothes ...'. The most important 'c' – capitalism – simply disappears from view in many such accounts. Another way of putting this point is that while there has been a great deal of interest in the *content* of contemporary citizenship, there has been very little questioning of its basic *form*. And yet, arguably the *content* of citizenship, what kinds of rights it encompasses or what groups may be excluded from its domain, has everything to do with its *form* – why 'contracts, constitutions, citizenship and civil society' take the form that they do and, more importantly, why the writ of democratic rights is limited in precisely the ways that it is in liberal capitalist societies. In other words, it doesn't really make sense to try to separate form from content since so much of the latter is conditioned by the former.

So, to query the form of capitalist citizenship is also to raise questions about the kind of method required to get behind the categories themselves, to ask after their historical origins and evolution over time. When Marx complained about the ahistorical method employed by the bourgeois political economists of his time, he was also making a point about their method of inquiry. Political economy ended up naturalizing the social relations of capitalism because it never once asked why, in Marx's words,

> labour power is expressed in value, and why the measurement of labour in duration is expressed in the magnitude of the value of the product. These formulas which bear the unmistakable stamp of belonging to a social formation in which the process of production has mastery over man, instead of the opposite, appear to the political economists' bourgeois consciousness to be as much a self-evident and nature-imposed necessity as productive labour itself.
>
> Marx (1977, 174–175)

As Patrick Murray (2003, 151) observes: 'The "illusion of the economic" usually takes the form of mistaking the capitalist mode of production for "production in general".' In other words, the central mistake of bourgeois political economy was to de-historicize and naturalize capitalist economic relations. We could say the same thing about what I will call the 'citizenship illusion': just as capital attempts to reify human labour in the form of value, so also does it seek to reify the bourgeois citizenship form as the *sine qua non* of human freedom.

Marx's dialectical method of inquiry was critical of reductive ways of thinking which reify and de-historicize complex social realities. 'Dialectical thinking allowed him to specify the "inner connections" of forms – contradictions, metamorphoses, "moments", immanent tendencies – in a way that structurally specified the possibilities for future development'

(Johnson 1982, 164). Abstraction was necessary, Marx believed, in order to unearth the inner structures and processes of capitalism. But not just any sort of abstraction would do. Bourgeois economics was rife with unhistorical abstractions which 'everywhere express the equality and freedom of the simple exchange of values: this point entirely reduces itself to an infantile abstraction' (quoted in Johnson 1982, 166).

Abstraction was necessary for an understanding of the 'inner connections' of capitalism because of the difference which exists between the way things appear from the standpoint of individual actors and the way things actually work at a systemic level. There is, in other words, a disjunction between essence and appearance. 'All science', Marx asserted, 'would be superfluous if the form of appearance of things directly coincided with their essence' (quoted in Lebowitz 2009, 70). We take this insight for granted in the physical sciences: few today would question the idea that the molecular structure of material objects may tell us a good deal more about the essential nature of things than is apparent when we hold the object in our hand. In the social sciences, however, the obvious truth of the distinction between appearance and essence is less apparent.

To put the argument another way, the necessary conditions for the reproduction of capitalism as a whole are different from those of individual actors taken separately.[4] The simplest illustration of this is when we consider that what is rational for the individual capitalist is generally not the case for the system as a whole. For example, the easiest way for an individual capitalist to make a profit would be simply to 'mark-up' the price of commodities above what it cost to produce them. This is indeed how some 'vulgar political economists' explained the origins of profit. Marx's (1977, 266) response to this argument was to say that while individuals could indeed capture extra surplus-value in this way, it was impossible for all producers to do so for the simple reason that they are also purchasers: 'The capitalist class of a given country, taken as a whole, cannot defraud itself.' The same logical fallacy repeats itself time and again. One of the founding myths of capitalism states that individual workers, through diligence and hard work, can become capitalists themselves. This is indeed the case for individuals but cannot be true for all workers; otherwise, there would be no labour to be exploited and therefore no capital or capitalists: 'The point is really very simple – the subject is the whole. The working class taken as a whole, the capitalist class taken as a whole, capitalism as a whole' (Lebowitz 2009, 7). Methodologies which proceed from particular cases to general theoretical axioms are bound to lead us in the wrong direction, to mistake surface appearance for essential relations and processes. Such notions persist, however, precisely because social formations constantly reproduce their own conditions of reproduction, often confusing the latter with the natural order of things: 'forms of appearance are reproduced directly and spontaneously, as current and usual modes of thought' (Marx 1977, 682). Thus, typical justifications of the profit system start by assuming as a *premise* or presupposition the supposedly natural human tendency towards greed and self-interest, which is in fact an *outcome* of capitalist social relations. This is why questioning the *form* taken by a given set of social relations necessarily pushes us towards enquiring after its historical preconditions.

In what follows, I attempt to map the '"inner connections" of forms' by means of the fundamental 'contradictions, metamorphoses, "moments" and immanent tendencies' of contemporary capitalism and imperialism. I try to link these forms with other social, political, subjective and even military forms and practices.[5] My intention, however foolhardy it might first appear, is not to collapse one social form into another as part of some grand folly of theoretical reductionism. Rather, my goal is to try to tease out the ways in which different aspects of our social world are mediated by more basic forms, such that seemingly disparate social 'facts' and 'discourses', upon closer inspection, turn out to be deeply connected parts of a larger whole. 'Only in this context', as the Hungarian Marxist George Lukács (1971, 8) asserted, 'which sees the isolated facts of social life as aspects of the historical process and integrates them in a *totality*, can knowledge of the facts hope to become knowledge of *reality*.'

To be sure, there are inherent dangers in such an exercise. If, as Fredric Jameson suggests, any attempt to 'cognitively map' the social totality of global capitalism today has become increasingly fraught because of the complexity of the system, it has also become much simpler in one crucial sense. The universalizing drive of capitalism means all of the social, economic and political forms we encounter are to some extent shaped by the imperatives of capitalism. And yet, much of the truth of this reality is repressed, displaced and reified by the structural contradictions of capitalism itself. To be able to 'think' the social forces now shaping our world necessarily means that we need to recuperate many of the abstract and universalizing modes of thought so widely spurned in the social sciences until recently (Eagleton 2003). Central to this endeavour is what Marx termed 'the force of abstraction', the temporary simplification and distillation of complex social realities in order to comprehend them more deeply. It is in the spirit of grasping our *present* reality in order that it may be radically transformed that the following account is offered.

My argument begins by tracing the historical preconditions of the form of capitalist citizenship for the way these preconditions shape both its form and content. I begin where Marx began in Volume One of *Capital* – with the commodity form. Marx begins with the commodity because he believed it expresses and condenses the *totality* of capitalist social relations. In other words, it is an analytical or conceptual starting point of the highest importance. Along the way, he also provides us with vital clues as to how this embryonic form gives rise to other social forms. One of these is the form which rights and liberties take in societies dominated by the commodity form. Building on these clues, I argue that the social form of citizenship in capitalist societies must be understood as a developed form of the commodity relation. Because the connections between the commodity form and the citizenship form are not merely conceptual but also material, I also try to map some of the subjective and ideological implications of their relationship. The chapter concludes with some reflections on how this framework might help us to understand the ways in which race and gender have been incorporated into liberal citizenship.

Chapter 2 takes a more contemporary tack by surveying the recent history of neo-liberal capitalism with an eye to how more developed forms of capital, such as credit and financialized capital, have also reshaped the basic parameters of liberal and less than liberal citizenship in the Global North and South. Chapter 3 examines this question from the standpoint of the 'new imperialism' and its relationship to neo-liberalism and the global economic crisis. While it is important to not reduce imperialism to its economic imperatives alone, it is equally important to situate it within the overall process of capitalist circulation. Given the centrality of finance capital in the global economy, it is not surprising that much of the vocabulary of 'securitization' and 'risk management' should also have found a home in the theory and practice of imperial warfare. The same language, I argue, has a lot to do with the way in which the apologists for empire conceive of the 'imperial subjects' they claim to be liberating. That these self-appointed liberators conceive of freedom in terms of political rights which are compatible with the market is not in doubt. But the labour regimes to which the new subjects of empire are submitted and the limited political rights that they enjoy are a far cry from conventional models of liberal citizenship. In this regard, the chapter concludes with a consideration of how the neo-liberal discourse of human rights has been mobilized not only as justification for imperial intervention but also as a further clue as to the kinds of political rights that the new subjects of empire – short of asserting their own views on the matter – might expect.

Chapter 4 pursues these themes in the realm of the security state itself. The national security state and the social security state that emerged in tandem during the Cold War rested on a model of full citizenship in which the general insecurity of wage-labour under capitalism would be compensated by a vast network of social security state-administered programmes. The breakdown of this social compact has seen a recasting of the meaning of 'security': while the state remains an active participant in risk management when it comes to such things as bank bailouts, natural disasters and military threats, social risks have been increasingly transferred from the state to individuals. A regime of public fear has amplified the general insecurities of work and life in a time of crisis; the spectral, phantom fears unleashed by the destructive powers of finance capital have found common cause with the 'war on terror'. The 'security fetish' (Neocleous 2008, 153) like the commodity fetish performs an ideological function by displacing and alienating human powers onto the objects and institutions of risk management. 'Securitized' citizenship, I contend, only heightens and amplifies its own fetishistic foundations: the more we invest in such alien sources of security, the more we increase the sources of our own alienation.

A final chapter considers perhaps the most important question all – the forms of resistance which have emerged to combat neo-liberal empire and the devastating consequences of austerity since 2008. While my comments are largely restricted to the situation in Latin America and focus mainly on the constraints of liberal citizenship, I hope that my summary of some of the key debates taking place among the region's Left will have a wider resonance.

Notes

1   I discuss in greater detail in Chapter 2 the historical ability of capitalism to adapt pre-capitalist forms of labour control and exploitation to suit its own needs.

2   See, J. M. Barbalet, *Citizenship: Rights, Struggle, and Class Inequality* (Milton Keynes: Open University, 1988). John Keane, *Civil Society and the State* (London: Verso, 1988); *Civil Society: Old Images, New Visions* (Stanford: Stanford University Press, 1998); Brian Turner, 'Contemporary Problems in the Theory of Citizenship', in Brian Turner and Thomas Janoski (eds.), *Citizenship and Civil Society* (Cambridge, England: Cambridge University Press, 1998).

3   For a good summary of postmodern politics, see Steven Best and Douglas Kellner, *The Postmodern Turn* (New York: The Guilford Press, 1997) 270–281.

4   Here I follow the arguments contained in the essays on method contained in Michael Lebowitz's collection, *Following Marx: Method, Critique, and Crisis* (Chicago: Haymarket Books, 2009).

5   It has been fashionable for some time in academia to dismiss such 'grand narratives', especially of the materialist variety advocated here. In its belief in self-subsistent 'discourses', post-structuralism and postmodernism

shared a common prejudice with a much older and more conservative form of methodological individualism in which only 'the facts' and not their interconnection to a greater whole were what mattered. One might have hoped that the events of 9/11, the rise of the Bush neo-cons, the invasions of Afghanistan and Iraq and the near collapse of the global financial system would have dampened some of these methodological certainties (Eagleton 2003).

1

Birth of the Liberal Subject: Commodities, Money and Citizenship

At the heart of capitalist social-property relations is the buying and selling of human labour. Capitalists purchase the creative capacities of workers in order to produce the commodities which are then sold in the market for profit. The 'secret' of this seemingly mundane social relation is that it is based upon an 'unequal exchange' between the capitalist and the worker. Simply put, workers produce more value for the capitalist than they receive in the form of a money wage. And, this surplus-value is ultimately the source of capitalist profit. Class exploitation, in other words, lies at the very centre of capitalist social-productive relations. It is a mark of how naturalized the buying and selling of human creative capacities has become that many people today seem to take it for granted. And yet, the commodification of human labour is key to the commodification of everything else and must have seemed as 'unnatural' at its origins as the buying and selling of water resources or human body parts seems to us today (McNally 2006, 40). It is worth considering these 'unnatural origins' in some detail.

Primitive accumulation

In Part 8 of *Capital*, Volume One, is a section titled 'On So-Called Primitive Accumulation' – 'so-called' because its actual history bears little resemblance to the 'nursery tale' to which classical political economy adheres. In Marx's (1977, 873) words, 'primitive accumulation plays approximately the same role in political economy as original sin does in theology'. In other words, classical political economy evacuates the actual history of the origins of capitalism into an unknowable mythological past. For Adam Smith, once upon an unspecified time certain more rational, frugal and ambitious individuals began to employ a greater mass of less rational, frugal and ambitious individuals who freely contracted with the former to sell their labour power. For John Locke, writing a century earlier, original accumulation was the happy result of the discovery of a non-perishable form of money, namely, gold. This allowed some (more rational) men to 'heap up as much of these durable things as he pleased, the exceeding of the bounds of his property not lying in the largeness of his possession but the perishing of anything uselessly in it' (Locke 1975, 28). In addition to providing a purported account of capitalism's origins, such formulations also provided the basic building blocks for liberal contract theory: not only were relations between buyers and sellers of labour power ostensibly free and equal, but the magic of money now justified unequal shares of the fruits of that labour. Left out of this account, Marx (1977, 874) wryly comments, is the 'notorious fact that conquest, enslavement, robbery, murder, in short, force, played the greatest part'.

As Marx explains, money and commodities are not inherently capital; they must be transformed into capital under specific historical conditions, namely, the coming together of two types of commodity owners: one with money and means of production, who seeks to increase the value of their property, and another, propertyless, with only their labour power to sell to others. But this relation between buyers and sellers of labour power did not come about by accident; rather, it was the result of a deliberate process of divorcing the producers from direct access to the means of subsistence: 'So-called primitive accumulation, therefore, is nothing else than the historical process of divorcing the producer from the means of production. It appears as "primitive" because it forms the pre-history of capital, and of the mode of production corresponding to capital' (Marx 1977, 874–875).

Marx's historical survey of primitive accumulation foregrounds the role of violence. 'Force', he tells us, 'is the midwife of every old society which is pregnant with a new one. It is itself an economic power' (Marx 1977, 916). This was nowhere more the case than in the European colonies where the thirst for gold and silver resulted in the decimation of indigenous societies:

The discovery of gold and silver in America, the extirpation, enslavement and entombment in the mines of the indigenous population of that continent, the beginnings of the conquest and plunder of India, and the conversion of Africa into a preserve for the commercial hunting of black skins, are all things which characterized the dawn of the era of capitalist production. This idyllic proceedings are the chief moments of primitive accumulation.

(Marx 1977, 915)

While Spain, Portugal, Holland and France had all profited from colonialism, by the seventeenth century only England was in a position to combine the proceeds of colonization and slavery with social changes already underway at home. In England, where, Marx (1977, 876) tells us, primitive accumulation 'has its classic form', the peasantry were gradually being driven off the land and into the ranks of wage-labour. On the other hand, the large farms were being consolidated, as huge tracts of common lands – which had been used for centuries for pasturage, wood gathering, fishing and game – were enclosed for private use. By the early decades of the nineteenth century, 'the commons' existed only in vestigial form; between 1700 and 1845, half the arable land in England, nearly six million acres, was subject to enclosure. Over the same period, it is reckoned that between 40,000 and 50,000 small farms were swallowed up by enclosures (Mooers 1991, 167–168).

Acts of Enclosure, it should be noted, were acts of the state; parliament simply expropriated peasant and common lands, annexing them to the great holdings of the landed classes. It helped, of course, that the English parliament during the eighteenth century, as described by Barrington Moore Jr. (1966, 19), was 'a committee of landlords'. To take a famous example, the Waltham Black Act of 1724 created at a single stroke fifty new capital offences governing poaching and game laws. As E.P. Thompson (1977, 206–207) remarked: 'The Act registered the long decline of the effectiveness of the old methods of class control and discipline and their replacement by one standard recourse of authority: the example of terror.'

English agriculture, now based on the classic triadic relation between great landlords who extracted rents from tenant farmers paying competitive rents, who in turn now employed wage-labour, was well established by the eighteenth century. Moreover, agricultural production was now thoroughly dependent on capitalist logics: maximizing exchange-values, cost-cutting and improvements in productivity, specialization, accumulation, reinvestment and innovation (Wood 2002, 125). Summing up the role of force and fraud in the historical trajectory of primitive accumulation in England, Marx concludes:

> The spoliation of the Church's property, the fraudulent alienation of the state domains, the theft of common lands, the usurpation of feudal and clan property and its transformation into modern private property under circumstances of ruthless terrorism, all these things were just so many idyllic methods primitive accumulation. They conquered the field for capitalist agriculture, incorporated the soil into capital, and created for the urban industries the necessary supply of free and rightless proletarians.
>
> Marx (1977, 895)

Nothing could be further from the anodyne story of capitalism's origins told by classical political economy. Money and machinery, in other words, are nothing without the essential ingredient of wage-labour; 'capital is not a thing, but a social relation between persons which is mediated through things' (Marx 1977, 932). 'Capital', Marx (1977, 926) reminds us, 'comes dripping from head to toe, from every pore, with blood and dirt.' However, extra-economic coercion is not necessary in quite the same way once capitalism has been fully established. Over many generations, the violent origins of capitalism are forgotten as workers become habituated to the impersonal and invisible coercion of market forces:

> The advance of capitalist production develops a working class which by education, tradition and habit looks upon the requirements of that mode of production as self-evident natural laws … once it is fully developed it breaks down all resistance … The silent compulsion of economic relations sets the seal on the domination of the capitalist over the worker. Direct extra-economic force is still of course used, but only in exceptional cases.
>
> Marx (1977, 899)

This passage appears to suggest that Marx wished to draw a sharp line between the violent origins of capitalism and the way it functions once capitalist market relations are fully established. As an historical account of a single country, this interpretation makes a good deal of sense. In England, by the final third of the nineteenth century, an independent peasantry was a distant memory; the majority of the working population were now employed as wage-labour subject to the 'silent compulsion of economic relations'. But this was not true of many European countries at the time. In France and Germany, small-scale agriculture remained dominant into the twentieth century and efforts at proletarianization were halting for many years to come. Capitalism, in other words, developed and continues to develop in a highly uneven geographical fashion. This fact has led those like David Harvey to propose that primitive accumulation is not a once and for all facet of capitalism's origins but an ongoing aspect of capitalist development *and* imperialism. On this view, the 'silent compulsion of economic relations' of advanced capitalism generates an ongoing necessity to resort to 'the idyllic methods of primitive accumulation'.

The apparent purpose of the section titled 'The Modern Theory of Colonization', which is inserted at the end of Marx's account of primitive accumulation, is to expose in the starkest terms the 'beautiful illusion' (Marx 1977, 935) of capitalism's origins in the contract between capital and labour. In his commentary on Edward Gibbon Wakefield's writings on colonization in the

Americas, Marx (1977, 932) explains that the 'great merit' of the work is 'to have discovered not something new *about* the colonies, but, *in* the colonies, the truth about capitalist relations in the mother country'. The central problem of the colonies, according to Wakefield (quoted in Marx 1977, 933), is that the settlers retain 'a passion for owning the land (which) prevents the existence of a class of labourers for hire'. While the worker holds on tenaciously to land and while the means of subsistence remain within his possession, capitalism cannot take root. Despite Wakefield's belief (quoted in Marx 1977, 933) that mankind had always naturally 'divided themselves into owners of capital and owners of labour', this had mysteriously not happened in the colonies. As Marx (1977, 934) acerbically notes, 'the mass of mankind expropriated itself in honour of the "accumulation of capital"'. The problem was a simple one: in a free colony, where land is plentiful (barring, of course, the claims of the indigenous people who may already claim it as their own), there was no incentive or desire to enter the ranks of wage-labour. As Wakefield laments (quoted in Marx 1977, 936), even when wage-labour is imported, no sooner have they taken advantage of the high wages on offer, than they 'cease ... to be labourers for hire; they ... become independent landowners, if not competitors with their former masters in the labour market'.

Harvey argues that there is a second, equally important, purpose to this lengthy commentary. Implicit in this text, he contends, is an understanding that capitalism is a dynamic system which constantly runs up against its own ability to absorb the massive surpluses that it produces. If crises of over-accumulation are to be avoided or at least attenuated, new outlets for productive investment must be found. One solution to this problem is to find a 'spatial fix' – a new geographical territory where capital and labour can be brought together to yield a profit. Historically, this has involved the export of capital overseas in search of new sources of labour, raw materials and markets:

> Geographical expansion of the productive forces therefore means expansion of the proletariat on a global basis ...The significance of that last chapter of the first volume of *Capital* now strikes home with redoubled force. The accumulation of capital is increase of the proletariat, and that means primitive accumulation of some sort or other.
>
> Harvey (1999, 436)

Primitive accumulation can take a variety of forms and may encounter a host of obstacles and, as we have seen, may combine both wage-labour and non-wage-labour forms. As we will see later on, this understanding of the link between the inner dynamics of capital accumulation and primitive accumulation is also important when we consider the nature of contemporary imperialism. It also highlights how the formation of 'imperial subjects' can assume a variety of social forms, ranging from the relatively privileged status enjoyed by citizens in the advanced capitalist states to states where much more repressive and limited-rights regimes exist. The latter may include not only countries which have been directly subjected to incursions of empire, such as Iraq or Afghanistan, but also those, like the rising state-capitalism of China, which have imposed one of the most radical programmes of primitive accumulation in history. Whether the Chinese path of authoritarian state-capitalism presents an image of capitalism's past or future remains to be seen.[1] For now, we need to clarify further the moment at which primitive accumulation gives rise to more fully developed capitalist social relations and where 'direct extra-economic force' has given way to the 'silent compulsion of economic relations'. For it is here, in the 'natural laws of production', that the liberal subject and 'all capitalism's illusions about freedom' are forged.

'Freedom, Equality, Property and Bentham'

When the buyers and sellers of labour power confront each other in the sphere of exchange, there is an apparent equality between capitalists and workers. The coercive aspects of market dependency – the fact that workers have no choice but to sell their labour having been deprived of means of subsistence of their own – have become naturalized and class inequality remains largely hidden from view. The sphere of exchange, as Marx (1977, 280) caustically observed, appears as 'a very Eden of the innate rights of man. It is the exclusive realm of Freedom, Equality, Property and Bentham'. This is not a minor point. What it suggests is that the creation of a market in human labour facilitated by the separation of economic and political powers signalled both the visible emergence of new freedoms as well as new and largely invisible forms of unfreedom. The formal equality which was to develop in most liberal-capitalist polities as time went on was closely allied to the formal appearance of equality between capitalists and workers in the marketplace. Indeed, as Marx (1977, 680) insightfully observed, the buying and selling of labour in the sphere of exchange is the source of this deceptive appearance: 'All notions of justice held by both the worker and the capitalist, all the mystifications of the capitalist mode of production, all capitalism's illusions about freedom, all the apologetic tricks of vulgar economics, have as their basis the form of appearance discussed above, which make the actual relation the invisible opposite of that relation'. Understanding the full implications of this observation, why it is that the 'form of appearance' of capitalist freedoms should necessarily 'make the actual relation the invisible opposite of that relation' is not immediately obvious. Why should capitalist social relations seem so opaque and why are our 'illusions about freedom' so difficult to decipher? Why, in other words, does the formal equality of the political sphere so often seem to overshadow the manifest class inequality of the economic sphere? For this, we need to turn to an analysis of Marx's theory of commodity fetishism and its specific implications for what I shall call the 'citizenship illusion'.

For Marx, the basis of these illusions was rooted in the commodity form itself. As he famously observes in the opening chapter of *Capital,* 'the commodity appears, at first sight, a very trivial thing, and easily understood. Its analysis shows that it is, in reality, a very queer thing, abounding in metaphysical subtleties and theological niceties' (1977, 163). Capitalist commodities embody three distinct but related types of value: use-value, value and exchange-value (Harvey 1999, 2). Under capitalism, concrete things – commodities – are produced by various types of concrete labours. Cars are made by a specific form of labour; software programmes by another. It matters not that one form of concrete labour is manual while the other involves intellectual, or what some have lately termed 'immaterial', labour. What Marx calls use-values represent the material and qualitative side of production and speak to the realm of human needs and wants. Qualitatively different use-values are employed for the satisfaction of different human purposes. However, for the capitalist, the primary interest in commodity production is not the use-value of the thing produced. He or she is interested primarily in the commodity's exchange-value against other commodities. But houses, coats and cars can only be exchanged against one another on the basis of some objective measure which is common to all the different forms of concrete labour involved in the production of these use-values. For Marx, the only possible objective basis for exchange is human labour-time. Thus, whatever use-value the commodity may have, it becomes possible to realize the value embodied in the commodity, as a definite quantity of labour-time, through its comparison with another use-value through an act of exchange. 'Socially necessary labour-time' is the average time it takes to produce a given commodity and not the actual time it may have taken to produce this or that commodity. What Marx terms 'abstract social labour' refers to the way in which socially necessary labour-time is expressed in quantitative terms as the measure of value. So every commodity has two sides, a use-value constituted through different acts of concrete labour and a value constituted by the amount of abstract social labour involved in its production. But value can only be realized through an act of exchange with another use-value; value can only be expressed as exchange-value.

The use-value of labour is unique in that it is the only commodity which is capable of producing more value in the time that it is employed than was paid for it; its use-value exceeds its exchange-value. The surplus-value which is produced through the deployment of labour power is the secret of capitalist profit. As Marx notes in the *Grundrisse*, 'in the exchange between capital and labour, it is precisely the use-value of the commodity purchased by the capitalist (i.e. labour-power) which constitutes the presupposition of the capitalist production process and the capital relation itself' (quoted in Rosdolsky 1977, 84). As much as capital would like to think of itself as self-subsistent, capable of infinite self-expansion without human intervention, it cannot escape its basis in the unique 'use-value' of human labour.

Here, it is important to stress Marx's insistence on the 'mutual opposition and mutual dependency' of use-value and exchange-value for reasons that shall become clear later.[2] For value to express itself through exchange, both poles need to be present. In section 3 of chapter 1 on 'The Commodity' in Volume One of *Capital*, Marx undertakes a detailed analysis of the complexities of the relative and equivalent forms of value. Here, Marx is at pains to demonstrate that value neither naturally inheres in the use-value of a commodity nor is it something which is created in the act of exchange. Exchange-value is 'the necessary mode of expression, or form of appearance of value' (Marx 1977, 128). Value, as a given quantity of socially necessary labour, is already present in the commodity; however, it can only 'appear in the social relation between commodity and commodity' (Marx 1977, 139). In the relative form of value, Marx explains, the value of a given quantity of linen is expressed through its relation to a second commodity, coats, expressed in the formula 20 yards of linen = one coat, or 20 yards of linen is worth one coat. Here, the socially necessary labour contained in the linen can only be expressed in the value of the material use-value of the coat. The value of the linen is expressed relative to coats. Therefore, the relative form of value presupposes that another commodity confronts it as an equivalent. At the same time, they are 'opposed extremes' (Marx 1977, 140) in that the commodity that serves as equivalent cannot at the same time be in the relative form and vice versa. In a suggestive metaphor, Marx (1977, 143) explains, 'In its value relation with the linen, the coat counts only under this (equivalent) aspect, counts therefore as embodied value, as the body of value … despite its buttoned up appearance, the linen recognizes in it a kindred soul, the soul of value.' What the equivalent form of value starkly reveals is 'that use-value becomes the form of appearance of its opposite, value … in the expression of value of the linen the coat represents a supra-natural property: their value, which is something purely social' (Marx 1977, 148–149).

Two things are important to note here. First, Marx has shown that value is not something which naturally inheres in use-values like its other material properties even though the equivalent form to some degree encourages this view. Second, he has shown that the dual-character of the commodity, as both use-value and exchange-value, exists in a mutually dependent and mutually contradictory relationship:

> The internal opposition between use-value and value, hidden within the commodity, is therefore represented on the surface by an external opposition, i.e. by a relation between two commodities such that the one commodity, *whose own* value is supposed to be expressed, counts directly only as a use-value, whereas the other commodity, *in which* that value is to be expressed, counts directly only as exchange-value. Hence, the simple form of value of a commodity is the simple form of appearance of the opposition between use-value and value which is contained within the commodity.
>
> Marx (1977, 153)

The commodity fetish

For Marx, the 'queer thing' about the commodity-form is that the social character of labour is obscured in the sphere of exchange, especially in the exchange which takes place between capital and labour. Rather, exchange-value seems to be something which inheres in the very use-value of the commodity itself. Things *appear* to govern relations between people:

> A commodity is therefore a mysterious thing, simply because in it the social character of men's labour appears to them as an objective character stamped upon the product of that labour; because the relation of the producers to the sum total of their own labour is presented to them as a social relation, existing not between themselves, but between the products of their labour. This is the reason why the products of labour become commodities, social things whose qualities are at the same time perceptible and imperceptible by the senses. In the same way the light from an object is perceived by us not as the subjective excitation of our optic nerve, but as the objective form of something outside the eye itself. But, in the act of seeing [...] [t]here is a physical relation between physical things. But it is different with commodities. There, the existence of the things *qua* commodities, and the value relation between the products of labour which stamps them as commodities, have absolutely no connection

with their physical properties and with the material relations arising there from. There it is a definite social relation between men, that assumes, in their eyes, the fantastic form of a relation between things. [...] This I call the Fetishism which attaches itself to the products of labour, so soon as they are produced as commodities, and which is therefore inseparable from the production of commodities.

Marx (1977, 83)

Social relations under capitalism thus have an inverted 'topsy-turvy' character identified by Marx with the commodity form of labour. In capitalism, there is an inversion of the relation between people and things such that things become subjectified and people become objectified: *the struggle to reify labour in value is what capital is all about* (Arthur 2003, 137). Thus, value, money and capital are 'spiritualized' to magically increase themselves independently of human intervention. In this sense, capitalism is just as much haunted by ghosts, spectres and phantoms as any pre-capitalist society.[3] In pre-capitalist societies, something of the spirit of the person was thought to be transferred to the artefact; under capitalism, just the opposite occurs: the embodied 'spirit' of the worker is exorcized from the object while the commodity is simultaneously re-animated with 'supra-sensible' value (Marx 1977, 165). This is the fundamental contrast between worlds where use-value and those where exchange-value predominates. By spiritualizing things and objectifying people, the commodity form 'inscribes *im*materiality as the defining feature of capitalism' (Stallybrass 1998, 184). At the same time, as it strips artefacts of the history, memory and desire with which concrete embodied labours invest them, capitalism refashions them into transcendental values – the spectral embodiments of appropriated labour – set free in phantom-form to roam the world.[4] These labours appear now only in the reified form of commodities and money, credit and finance – as alien objects which betray nothing of their origins. As David McNally summarizes:

[C]ommodity-fetishism at its deepest level is a religion of *non-sensuous* desire. However much capitalists bow down before things, their true god is immaterial. Rather than desire for things for their material properties, capitalists actually seek that invisible and immaterial property they share: value. After all, it is only their property as products of human labour in the abstract, labour stripped of all material specificity which makes commodities commensurable and exchangeable with money. But this means that value, the entity worshipped by capitalists, is entirely invisible, intangible, an actual power whose objectivity is purely phantasmal.

McNally (2011, 127)

For the 'subjects' of capitalism, these social forms are bound up with specific types of subjectivity and consciousness – modes of signification and 'structures of feeling' which shape and limit our ways of understanding and acting on the world. There exists, in other words, an *immanent* relationship between social form and subjective content. This means that our ideas are embedded in social and material practices such that our views about what is politically possible are powerfully conditioned by the kinds of social structures and forms we inhabit. The fetishistic form of capitalist social relations encourages forms of subjectivity and ways of thinking about the world which systematically misrepresent and distort social reality. As Lukács (1975, 83) put it at the beginning of his famous 1920 essay 'Reification and the Consciousness of the Proletariat', 'the riddle of the commodity-*structure*' must be considered 'the central, structural problem of capitalist society in all its aspects. Only in this case can the structure of commodity-relations be made to yield a model of all the objective forms of bourgeois society together with all the subjective forms corresponding to them'. Fetishistic thinking is embedded in fetishistic social relations and practices. While Lukács tends to overdraw the 'nature-like automaticity' between capitalism's reifying logic and 'subjective forms' (Albritton 2003, 63), he is surely correct in emphasizing the fundamental role which the commodity form plays in shaping human consciousness. Whatever else might be involved in the formation of human subjectivity from a psychoanalytic point of view, it is undeniably the case that a large part of the grammar of signification (Knafo 2002) in capitalist society – the way we apprehend social reality – depends upon the distorting effects of the commodity form; the inversions involved in commodity fetishism both limit and 'decentre' our subjective understanding of the world.

This is most obviously the case when we enter the market as apparently autonomous actors. The impersonality of the market, with its quantitative and monetized character, encourages the belief that its operations are somehow objective and natural. Rather than seeing the market as an artefact of historically specific set of social relations, we experience it as an external force governed by the actions of things. So, we try to make sense of the world in terms of commodities and money as though they were the timeless arbiters of human interactions.

Money and social abstraction

The historical emergence of the value-form was for Marx (1977, 167) the key to deciphering the 'social hieroglyphic' of capitalist social relations. Indeed, for Marx, the value-form was crucial for the development of notions of human equality which arose in tandem with capitalism:

The secret of the expression of value, namely the equality and equivalence of all kinds of labour could not be deciphered until the concept of human equality had already acquired the permanence of a fixed popular opinion. This however becomes possible only in a society where the commodity-form is the universal form of the product of labour, hence the dominant social relation between men as possessors of commodities.

Marx (1977, 152)

Money, in its various modalities, would also prove uniquely compatible with the abstract civic and political forms peculiar to modern capitalism. Although money was not invented by capitalism, its role in capitalist society plays several key functions. Money's primary role is to serve as a universal equivalent by means of which exchange-values can be equalized and through which value can be expressed. Money also serves as a means of circulating and storing value and as a means of payment. So, like every other commodity, money has both an exchange-value and a use-value (Harvey 1999, 11–12). It matters not that the money-commodity is made of precious metal, paper currency, credit, 'securitized' assets or digital impulses; these are merely different forms (use-values) of the money-commodity for expressing and embodying value. For Marx, what is important about the money-form is that it condenses and mediates the fundamentally *alienated* social relations of capitalism. In his observations on James Mill's 1821 *Elements of Political Economy*, Marx (1844) characterizes the 'soul of money' in the following terms:

The complete domination of the estranged thing *over* man has become evident in *money*, which is completely indifferent both to the nature of the material, i.e., to the specific nature of the private property, and to the personality of the private property owner. What was the domination of person over person is now the general domination of the *thing* over the *person*, of the product over the producer. Just as the concept of the *equivalent*, the value, already implied the *alienation* of private property, so *money* is the sensuous, even objective existence of this *alienation*.

Money is the ultimate fetish because of its ability to order social relationships between people *as if* this was one of its natural attributes, rather than the other way around – that money takes the form it does as a measure of abstract social labour *because* social production is organized along capitalist lines. Under capitalism, Marx (1973, 157) famously remarks in the *Grundrisse*, the 'individual carries his social power, as well as his bond with society, in his pocket'. He was referring here to the fact that whatever other uses money had, it was the pre-eminent expression of social power and wealth. The circulation of money conditions virtually every aspect of life, from the money we receive in the form of wages to that spent on food, shelter, education, entertainment, old age, births and deaths (Zelizer 1994, 202). How, and under what circumstances, we do these things largely depends on our social relationship to money. This is not meant to imply that money is a thing external to the social relations that constitute it. Indeed, it was the burden of Marx's analysis to demonstrate that money embodies both the freedom afforded by monetary wealth and the unfreedom entailed by the earning of it through alienated labour. As Bertell Ollman (1988, 84–85) observes:

> money is understood as the power without which nothing is possible, so that greed for money becomes perfectly rational; being allowed to do anything for money when you need some and buy whatever you want to when you have some serves as the paradigm for freedom (the market mystifies freedom making one believe that one can do what one can't, and, when one does what one can, it makes one believe that one has done what one hasn't); equality is when others can do the same ...

In historical terms, the generalization of the money-form represents the triumph of social abstraction over older, more direct and transparent relations of domination and dependence. Henceforth, both political life and subjective conceptions of the social world would be powerfully shaped by the forces of *real abstraction* inherent in the money-form. But the money-form also intensifies the misrecognition of social reality; as social relations become more abstract, they also become increasingly opaque.

Alfred Sohn-Rethel was one of the first Marxist thinkers to explore the relationship between what he termed *real abstractions* inherent in the commodity-form, money and human subjectivity. He rejects Immanuel Kant's notion, set out in the *Critique of Pure Reason*, that consciousness is rooted in an *a priori* set of transcendental categories of mind.[5] According to Sohn-Rethel, the distinctive thing about human subjectivity, especially the capacity for abstract thought, is precisely its historical character. For him, the abstract categories of thought only emerge in societies based on commodity exchange and monetized social relations:

> the 'transcendental unity of self-consciousness', to use the Kantian expression for the phenomenon here involved, is itself an intellectual reflection of one of the elements of the exchange abstraction, the most fundamental one of all, the form of exchangeability of the commodities

underlying the unity of money and of social synthesis. I define the Kantian 'transcendental subject' as a fetish concept of the capital function of money.

Sohn-Rethel (1978, 77)

Theodor Adorno (2000, 177) later emphasized the profound implications of Sohn-Rethel's rejection of the Kantian paradigm for understanding the social nature of consciousness:

Alfred Sohn-Rethel was the first to point out that hidden in this principle, in the general and necessary activity of the mind, lies the work of an inalienably social nature. The aporetical concept to act, a universal which is nonetheless to have particular experiences – would be a soap bubble, never obtainable from the autarkic immanent context of consciousness, which is necessarily individual. Compared with consciousness, however, the concept represents not only something more abstract; by virtue of its coining power it also represents something more real. Beyond the magic circle of identitarian philosophy, the transcendental subject can be deciphered as a society unaware of itself. Ever since mental and physical labor were separated in the sign of the dominant mind, the sign of justified privilege, the separated mind has been obliged, with the exaggeration due to a bad conscience, to vindicate the very claim to dominate which it derives from the thesis that it is primary and original – and to make every effort to forget its claim, lest the claim lapse.

In Sohn-Rethel's view, 'the exchange abstraction' is characteristic of societies based on commodity production and money. Only where money functions as the universal equivalent does it perform 'its socially synthetic function', binding widely dispersed social actors together in a cohesive network of social relations:

In this capacity money must be vested with an abstractness of the highest level to enable it to serve as the equivalent of every kind of commodity that may appear on the market. This abstractness of money does not appear as such and cannot be expected to 'appear' as it consists of nothing but form – pure abstract form arising from the disregard of the use-value of commodities operated by the act of exchange equating the commodities as values … these constituent elements of the exchange abstraction unmistakably resemble the conceptual elements of the cognitive faculty emerging with the growth of commodity production.

Sohn-Rethel (1978, 6)

Sohn-Rethel (1978, 25) insists that 'the salient feature of the act of exchange is that its separation from use has assumed the compelling necessity of an objective social law. Wherever commodity exchange takes place, it does so in effective "abstraction" from use'. Sohn-Rethel (1978, 27) thus draws a sharp line between use-value, which he defines solely in terms of 'man's interchange with nature' and exchange which 'is purely social by its constitution and scope'. The social bond which results from exchange, as well as the abstract and universal principles of social organization and thought to which it gives rise, can only take place through 'enforcing the separation from use, or more precisely from the actions of use … devoid of all inter-exchange of man with nature' (Sohn-Rethel 1978, 29). Echoing this view, Slavoj Žižek (2000, 105) has more recently observed:

> [I]n a society in which commodity exchange predominates, individuals themselves in their daily lives, relate to themselves, as well as the objects they encounter, as to contingent embodiments of abstract-universal notions. What I am, my concrete social or cultural background is experienced as contingent, since what ultimately defines me is the 'abstract' universal capacity to think and/or work … 'abstraction' becomes a direct feature of actual social life, the way concrete individuals behave and relate to their fate and to their social surroundings.

While acknowledging the importance of these insights for understanding the relationship between 'real abstraction' and consciousness, it is also essential to recall the 'mutual opposition and mutual dependency' of use-value and exchange-value. Sohn-Rethel effectively de-socializes use-value by associating it with humanity's interactions with nature. In doing so, he loses sight of the fact that value originates not in exchange *per se* but through the production of abstract social labour; it is not the 'exchange abstraction' in the sphere of circulation which is the key, but rather the commodity abstraction which takes place in the sphere of production (Jappe 2013, 10).

It is worth emphasizing this point chiefly because many theorists influenced by postmodernism have tended to treat the relationship between use-value and exchange-value as a purely arbitrary construction. This has led to a rejection of the so-called 'labour metaphysic', the idea that the secret of value lies in 'precisely the use-value of the commodity purchased by the capitalist (i.e. labour-power)' and, therefore, of the task of unravelling the mystifications and contradictions of capitalism itself. As a consequence, it has led to an exaggeration of the 'rule of exchange-value' and by extension, to a serious misreading of contemporary social and political forms. As Gail Day (2011, 216–217) explains:

Marx takes economic forms to be the clearest indices of the historical changes to the organization of social relations. His concern is to establish where and how categories often assumed as transhistorical specifically operated within – or determinate for – generalized commodity production. The historical specificity of exchange value's dominance is widely accepted today, but use-value's disappearance is often taken, mistakenly, to be the corollary ... However, when considered from the perspective of form – more precisely, when considered as a determinate social form – use value becomes critically important in the case of two highly significant commodities: the money commodity and labor power.

The contradictory unity of use-value and exchange-value also has important theoretical consequences for understanding the reified and fetishistic character of the capitalist form of citizenship. Commodity abstraction makes it possible to *conceive* of civic status in terms of abstract notions of equality and freedom but in a manner which systematically obscures the origins of these abstractions. So, for example, as Bonefeld (1995, 187–188) argues, there exists a homology between the money-form and the form of abstract citizenship peculiar to bourgeois societies: 'Money represents the standardization of individuals as abstract citizens ... Money is the incarnation of liberty, of private property. It represents the liberty of individualized property owners, their equality and freedom.' Moreover, the money fetish (as the universal equivalent of abstract social labour) becomes the basis for a whole host of juridic and political fetishisms. The ownership of private property (including the worker's property in his or her own labour), contractual relations, equality before the law and the state all appear to be the result of human nature or disinterested reason (Fine 1986, 97–98; Mooers 2001, 62).[6] Just as the commodity form conceals the human labours which went into its production, so too does the form of capitalist citizenship obscure the class antagonisms which lie below its surface. Thus, the systematic distortion of social reality associated by Marx with the fetishism of commodities now encompasses the gamut of social relations under capitalism, from wage relations to its most developed juridical and political forms.

Ideology and the citizenship illusion

The subjection of labour to the rule of capital has been, above all, about subjection to market imperatives and the formation of a legal-subject with specific rights and obligations. This meant the creation of an abstract legal subject 'as the bearer of every imaginable legal claim' (Pashukanis 118). In his *General Theory of Law and Marxism* (1929), Evgeny Pashukanis traces the origins of the legal subject to the rise of the capitalist commodity form. Following Marx, Pashukanis (1978, 117) suggests that legal subjectivity is the fetishistic form of legal relations which mirrors and reproduces at the legal and political level the fetishistic character of the commodity form: '... the social relations of production assume a doubly mysterious form ... they appear as relations between things (commodities) and ... as relations between the wills of autonomous entities equal to each other – of legal subjects'.

In other words, commodity fetishism was not just about the mystification of social relations in the realm of production; it was also key to a whole host of other forms of social fetishism, including that which exists between ostensibly equal, abstract legal subjects. Legal subjectivity in the sense implied by Pashukanis has to do with the basic form of abstract citizenship and its relationship to the commodity form of labour. The state and judiciary are of course central to the definition of legal subjectivity. But like the 'autonomous entities' it constitutes as formally equal citizens, the state too appears to stand above the fray as an autonomous and impartial force. This is so, as Pashukanis (1978, 141) observes,

> firstly because we have here a special apparatus, separate from the representatives of the ruling class, which stands above every individual capitalist and functions as an impersonal force. Secondly ... this impersonal force does not mediate every individual exploitative relation; the wage worker is not actually politically and legally *compelled* to work for a *particular* entrepreneur; rather, he formally sells that entrepreneur his labour power on the basis of a free contract. In so far as the exploitative relation exists formally as a relationship between two 'autonomous' and 'equal' owners of commodities, of whom one, the proletarian, sells his labour power, and the other, the capitalist, buys it, political class power can take on the form of a public authority.

Thus, the commodity form of labour is directly related to the production of forms of subjectivity which are necessary for the citizenship illusion to work. More recently, Paul Smith has revealingly referred to this form of subjectivity as the 'subject of value' to denote its affinity with the value-form of abstract labour. 'Subjects of value' are defined by three basic principles: 'it is (1) endowed with an ultimately self-interested rationality, (2) convinced of the principle of equality, and (3) dedicated to the principle of private property' (Smith 2007, 30). Each of these principles promotes a cluster of beliefs, desires and behaviours suited to the accumulation of capital through the exploitation of human labour. They are also at the core of the citizenship illusion. As we have seen, classical political economy and, to the degree that it is any longer interested in such questions, most of mainstream economics assume that 'possessive individualism' is a natural disposition which capitalism just happened to stumble upon. The fact that it took several millennia for this to occur should alert us to the fact that we are not talking about natural dispositions at all but rather a change in historical circumstances which allowed certain appetites to flourish while extinguishing others. Once producers were deprived of direct access to the means of subsistence and once owners of property became subject to market competition – once all needs and desires became mediated by the market – acquisitiveness, calculation and self-interest were bound to become the measure of rationality.

The principle of equality might at first appear at odds with this picture of capitalist reality. But, as we saw earlier, the appearance of equality is built into the very fabric of the relations of exchange. Even though it is obvious that capitalism results in dramatic inequalities, it is a cornerstone of liberal ideology that everyone at least begins from the same starting point. As with the sanctity of private property, this precept has broad appeal not just for capitalists but, to a limited degree, for workers as well. After all, workers are constantly enjoined to see their own labour as a form of private property which they contract to sell to the capitalist for a money wage. The actual inequality involved in this transaction is both a product of an unseen history of dispossession and enclosure which produced the modern wage relation in the first place and the fetishized form which that relation takes under capitalism. Subjectively, material conditions encourage workers to forget both history and reality and to see themselves as equal participants and beneficiaries of the system of private property and free contractual relations. As Smith (2007, 32) observes:

> the subject of value, understanding equality and freedom as more or less synonymous, must be able to forget the history that gives rise to alienation and must be able to elide the empirical evidence of inequality. The subject of value thus cleaves to factitious rights of equality in spite of empirical effects of capital's freedom. The subject of value is ex-historical in that sense.

To suggest that commodities, money and citizenship are connected forms of fetishism is not to imply that they are *mere* illusions or the product of some sort of 'false-consciousness'. Indeed, Žižek (1989, 31) has suggested that the ideological force of money rests not in its 'falsity' but rather in our willingness to *act* as if the money-illusion were true:

When individuals use money, they know very well that there is nothing magical about it – that money, in its materiality, is simply an expression of social relations. The everyday spontaneous ideology reduces money to a simple sign giving the individual possessing it a right to a certain part of the social product. So, on an everyday level, the individuals know very well that there are relations between people behind the relations between things. The problem is that in their social activity itself, in what they are *doing*, they are *acting* as if money, in its material reality, is the embodiment of wealth as such. They are fetishists in practice, not in theory.

Thus, the twin fetishisms of money and citizenship are not forms of 'false consciousness' so much as spontaneous forms of consciousness which arise out of a contradictory social reality which is itself based on an 'objectified illusion' (Hawkes 1996, 177) rooted in the structural contradictions of capitalism itself:

Ideology is not some dreamlike illusion that we build to support an insupportable reality; in its basic dimension it is a fantasy-construction which serves as a support for our 'reality' itself: an 'illusion' which structures our effective, real social relations and thereby masks some insupportable, real, impossible kernel … .

Žižek (1989, 45)

So, it is perhaps more accurate, then, to think of the discourse of citizenship as something like a 'compromise formation', as in Freud's account of neurotic behaviour. As Terry Eagleton (1991, 134) has suggested:

The 'truth' of such ideology, as with the neurotic symptom, lies neither in the revelation nor the concealment alone, but in the contradictory unity they compose. It is not just a matter of stripping off some outer disguise to expose the truth, any more than an individual's self-deception is just a 'guise' he assumes. It is rather that what is revealed takes place in terms of what is concealed and *vice versa*.

Why citizenship rights have the character of a 'compromise formation' is rooted in the dual-sided nature of wage-labour itself. On the one hand, as owners of their own labour power, workers are also property-owners of a certain type. Capitalist notions of property rights are bound to have some appeal since, in the limited sense that they enjoy 'property in their persons' as Locke liked to say, they dispose of their labour power as the *apparent* equal of the capitalist who purchases it. The money wage which the worker receives is fraught with social meaning. It invites the worker into the 'community of money' as an apparently equal participant in the appropriation of the fruits of private property and freely contracted relationships (Harvey 1985, 4).[7] In terms of political consciousness, the dual nature of wage-labour means that workers are pushed to struggle against the limitations of capital as well as being pulled by its apparent attractions. The role of money expresses these contradictory impulses clearly as a 'tension between the individualism that attaches to the spending of money and the class experience of earning that splits the social and psychological foundations for political action' (Harvey 1985, 33). This means that the individualistic norms which govern the world of monetary exchange often tend to overshadow class-based demands. Since human needs are mediated by the market it is not surprising that the idioms of the market should become the 'common sense' to which most people adhere most of the time. Money, within definite constraints, really does afford a degree of individual autonomy and freedom. Like money, therefore, the circumscribed citizenship rights of capitalism are a *practical* fetish: people are aware of their limits, just as they know that such rights are often subverted by money and power. But, much of the time, they *act* as if this was not the case.

Race, gender and citizenship[8]

Historically, modern forms of racism and gender inequality have been deeply imbricated with capitalist processes of colonialism, capital accumulation and labour migration (Harvey 2000; Miles and Brown 2003). Modern biological racism was the product of two conflicting tendencies. On the one hand, the advent of free wage-labour was one of the fundamental building blocks of political democracy. The doctrine espoused by all of the major liberal theorists starts from the premise that human beings are born equal. On the other hand, colonial expansion and the slave trade had underwritten early capitalist accumulation to a considerable degree. The dilemma is obvious: how was it possible to justify the enslavement of millions and remain consistent with the principles of liberal theory? This was precisely the question posed by Toussaint L'Ouverture and the slave rebellion in Haiti that erupted in the wake of the French Revolution. To the cries of '*Liberté, Égalité, Fraternité*' echoing from the revolutionary assemblies in Paris, Toussaint replied: 'I want liberty and equality in San Domingo' (Blackburn 1988, 218). It was arguably this contradiction that produced the nineteenth-century ideology of racial inferiority – a doctrine which allowed for the cohabitation of the liberal ideals of formal equality and freedom among 'equals' and racial inequality and unfreedom for those considered less than fully human. But as Wood points out, 'it was precisely the structural pressure *against* extra-economic difference made it necessary to justify slavery by excluding slaves from the human ͻ, making them non-persons standing outside the normal universe of freedom and equality' (Wood 1995, 269).

But capitalism also has an uncanny ability to absorb forms of oppression inherited from the past, which it interweaves with newer configurations of race and gender to produce baroque ideologies of the body. With the rise of what Anne McClintock has called 'commodity imperialism' in the late nineteenth century,

> the rhetoric of race was used to invent distinctions between what we would now call *classes*...the rhetoric of *gender* was used to make increasingly refined distinctions among the *races*. The White race was figured as the male of the species and the black race as the female. Similarly, the rhetoric of *class* was used to inscribe minute and subtle distinctions between other *races*.
>
> McClintock (1995, 54–55)

In capitalist society, human labour is seen as the product of non-bourgeois others. Bourgeois society is characterized by 'its othering of the body and its embodying of others' (McNally 2001, 4). The effacement of concrete bodily labours produced a dialectic of embodiment and hyper-embodiment in which the reproductive labours of women (in the form of both domestic and procreative labour) and the forced and sweated labours of the colonized and exploited were excluded from recognition within the public sphere. Reduced to their bodies, these groups have been sexualized as mothers and fantasy objects or as racialized subjects on whose bodies are inscribed discourses of animal and sexual desire. Labouring bodies of all sorts are effaced in 'grand narrative' of bourgeois society while its cultural achievements are spiritualized as the accomplishments of great thinkers and statesmen.

The circulation of variable capital in the form of wage-labour reconstructs race and gender in specifically capitalist ways (Harvey 2000). There exists an 'interplay between the social relations of production and the racialization process' (Miles and Torres 1999, 33). Race is a signifying practice that permits the construction of racial hierarchies and divisions within the labour process. As San Juan observes:

> The capitalist mode of production articulated 'race' with class in a peculiar way... In the capitalist development of U.S. society, African, Mexican, and Asian bodies – more precisely, their labor power and its reproductive efficacy were colonized and racialized.... 'Race' is thus constructed out of

raw materials furnished by class relations, the history of class conflicts, and the vicissitudes of colonial/capitalist expansion and the building of imperial hegemony. It is dialectically accented and operationalized not just to differentiate the price of wage labor within and outside the territory of the metropolitan power, but also to reproduce relations of domination-subordination invested with an aura of naturality and fatality. The refunctioning of physical or cultural traits as ideological and political signifiers of class identity reifies social relations. Such 'racial' markers enter the field of the alienated labor process concealing the artificial nature of meanings and norms, and essentializing or naturalizing historical traditions and values which are contingent on mutable circumstances.

San Juan (2003, 13–14)

Class, then, is always raced and gendered: 'it cannot be understood independently of concrete social relations which specify the concretizing forms of difference' (Bannerji 1995, 34). Concrete labour is *embodied* labour in the fullest sense of the term. It is at the point of production where concrete bodies are most immediately and sentiently present and where the realities of racism and gender discrimination become palpable. It is here that the conjunction of class, race and gender becomes a *lived* experience, for it is here that specific labours are bound up with specific groups of individuals. And, it is also here that the myriad humiliations and degradations of racism and sexism are meted out: scapegoating, targeting, excessive monitoring, marginalization, infantilization, segregation, blaming the victim and tokenism (Das Gupta 1996, 35–40).

Citizenship within the classical bourgeois public sphere was conceived as essentially white and masculine; it implicitly assumed the bourgeois male as the universal class (Fraser 1996). Its presupposition, in other words, entailed the exclusion of women, the working class and racialized others who did not correspond to the bourgeois masculine ideal. If citizenship within the public sphere was the realm of abstract generality in which concrete particularities were to be left behind, the private sphere was conceived as 'the realm of affectivity, affiliation, need and the body' (Young 1998, 406). Thus, in the bourgeois public sphere, the 'virile subject' (Oliver 1997, 119) of the white, bourgeois male became the repository for abstract authority, property and the law. Those who are deemed to have control *over* their bodies become full citizens, whereas those who are ruled *by* their bodies become lesser citizens (Bacchi and Beasley 2002). As Lauren Berlant observes:

white male privilege has been veiled by the rhetoric of the bodiless citizen, the generic 'person' whose political identity is *apriori* precisely because it is, in theory, noncorporeal...The white, male body is the relay to legitimation, but even more than that, the power to suppress that body, to cover its tracks and its traces, is the sign of real authority, according to constitutional fashion.

Berlant (1993, 176)

Concrete bodies are simultaneously suppressed and acquire a 'surplus corporeality of racialized and gendered subjects' (178).

Thus, the capitalist separation between private and public can be understood in terms of a dialectics of bodily exclusion and hyper-embodiment of those whose labours are the source of its material and cultural achievements. On the one hand, the abstract generality of citizenship within the public sphere requires that all concrete, corporeal markers of identity be left behind; on the other, these same bodies are 'marked' by configurations of class, race and gender. In other words, the dialectic of embodiment present in the bourgeois public sphere may equally be seen as a mediated form of capitalism's basic social-productive relations – relations which simultaneously ascribe differential value to different types of concrete labour and deny this reality at the level of market exchange through the formal appearance of equality.

What then, are we to make of contemporary policies of racial and gender diversity and multicultural citizenship adopted by many liberal capitalist states? First, it must be emphasized that any recognition which oppressed and excluded groups receive in the public sphere is an important achievement, especially when recognition has been forced upon the state by popular struggles from below. But, it is also true that such policies were often conceived and implemented from above as a means of managing diversity in the wake of the successive waves of labour migration to the metropoles in the post-colonial period. They were also seen as a way of containing and neutralizing many of the more radical claims of the anti-racist movements of the late 1960s and 1970s which, in some instances, had begun to intersect with those of class. With the language of 'diversity' 'the concept of race lost its hard edges of criticality, class disappeared entirely, and colour gave a feeling of brightness, brilliance or vividness, of a celebration of difference which was disconnected from social relations of power, but instead perceived as diversity, as existing socio-cultural ontologies or facts' (Bannerji 2000, 32).

If, in the classical liberal public sphere, it is the white, bourgeois male which lurks behind the opaque form of abstract citizenship, with multicultural citizenship a new twist presents itself: the racialized body is brought back in, only this time as a *visible* abstraction. *Visibility* functions as a form of concealment through the relentless exposure of embodied difference. Visible hyper-embodiment becomes the 'fantastic form' which conceals racism at the heart of the system; a 'phantasmagoria' of difference. The fetishism at work here is one which operates at the level of what appears to be a relation between concrete individuals but which is in fact a reified abstraction; the mystification, paradoxically, rests in the laying bare of visible difference. The 'paradox of diversity', identified by Bannerji, takes precisely this form: 'the concept of diversity simultaneously allows for an emptying out of actual social relations and suggests a concreteness of cultural description and through this process obscures any understanding of difference as a construction of power' (Bannerji 2000, 36).

Liberal multiculturalism, therefore, partakes in its own form of fetishism. The reified ethnicities which underlie it involve a specific kind of inverted reality based in a quite distinct dialectic of revelation and concealment. Multiculturalism conceals the racialization and gendering of concrete social relations behind the surface appearance of domesticated, bearable otherness: the hyper-visibility of 'visible minorities' and 'people of colour' becomes the camouflage which masks the racism at the core of capitalism – hidden, as it were, in plain sight. Multicultural citizenship, therefore, conceals as much as it reveals. The trick is that it does this through the exposure of difference. In this sense, multicultural visibility has become part of the phantasmagoria of late capitalism where 'universal visibility ... is welcomed and reveled in for its own sake' (Jameson 1998, 110). The 'brightness, brilliance and vividness' of diversity become allied to the general consumption of images which distinguishes contemporary commodity culture. Ultimately, this is why the 'otherness' represented in multiculturalism seems so familiar – because it has been so effectively assimilated to the commodity form. Saturated with the logic of the commodity form, multiculturalism is really a variant of what Adorno called 'identity thinking', which, in this case, seeks to reduce otherness to a simulacrum of itself or, alternately, expel it in a paranoid act of exclusion. As a form of 'identity thinking' it homogenizes the world while cleverly presenting itself as a radical difference. Like the social system from which it springs, it presents the ever-same in the form of the ever-different. As such, liberal multiculturalism is an ideology of denial. It asks the oppressed to make an affective investment in the reified ethnicities it establishes and to forget those bodily memories of racism which rear up from everyday life but which now find no place in the official transcript of the public sphere. Liberal multiculturalism amplifies the fetishistic form of liberal citizenship through its own peculiar dialectic of revelation and concealment by effacing the lived experience of racism (and sexism) through the apparent validation of visible forms of difference. In effect, its message to the oppressed is 'your difference is now acknowledged; you are part of the colourful tapestry of the nation', and, implicitly, 'so stop whining about racism'.

Notes

1 Slavoj Žižek (2008) has suggested the latter:

> What if the promised second stage, the democracy that follows the authoritarian vale of tears, never arrives? This, perhaps, is what is so unsettling about China today: the suspicion that its authoritarian capitalism is not merely a reminder of our past – of the process of capitalist accumulation which, in Europe, took place from the 16th to the 18th century – but a sign of our future? What if the combination of the Asian knout and the European stock market proves economically more efficient than liberal capitalism? What if democracy, as we understand it, is no longer the condition and motor of economic development, but an obstacle to it?

2 For one of the clearest and most insightful discussions of this point, see Gail Day, *Dialectical Passions: Negation in Postwar Art Theory* (New York: Columbia University Press, 2011) 213–217.

3 For a fascinating discussion of this point, see (McNally, 2012).

4 As Michael Taussig (1993, 22–23) observes:

> We need to note … that as the commodity passes through and is held by the exchange-value arc of the market circuit where general equivalence rules the roost, where all particularity and sensuosity is meat-grinded into abstract identity and the homogeneous substance of quantifiable money-value, the commodity yet conceals in its innermost being not only the mysteries of the socially constructed nature of value and price, but also all its particulate sensuousity – and this subtle interaction of sensuous perceptibility and imperceptibility accounts for the fetish quality, the animism and spiritual glow of commodities … .

5 In section two of that work, Kant (1965, 155) writes:

> I am conscious of the self as identical in respect of the manifold of representations that are given to me in an intuition, because I call them one and all *my* representations, and so apprehend them as constituting *one* intuition. This amounts to saying that I am conscious to myself *a priori* of a necessary synthesis of representations – to be entitled the original synthetic unity of apperception – under which all representations that are given to me must stand, but under which they have also first to be brought by means of synthesis.

6 For an extended discussion of law and the state as *forms* of capitalist social relations, see Simon Clarke (1991); Werner Bonefeld, Richard Gunn and Kosmas Psychopedis (1992; 1995); John Holloway (2002).

7 The 'community of money' affects the *form* of citizenship in other ways.
   It was Simmel (1990, 300), following Marx, who recognized that a money
   economy establishes a relationship of abstract indifference between citizens
   which closely parallels the abstract character of money: '… the inhabitants
   of a modern metropolis are independent in the positive sense of the
   word, and, even though they require innumerable suppliers, workers and
   cooperators … their relationship to them is completely objective and is only
   embodied in money'. It was this social distancing effect of money relations
   which Simmel (1990, 255) saw as the source of the blasé attitude and
   cynicism of modern life. The most prolific 'nurseries of cynicism' were in his
   view 'stock exchange dealings where money is available in huge quantities
   and changes owners easily' (Simmel 1990, 256).

8 What follows draws on sections from a previous publication. See Mooers
   (2006a).

2

States of Insecurity: From Social Rights to Social Debts

The neo-liberal counter-revolution

The neo-liberal revolution which began in the early 1970s in the aftermath of the first major recession of the post-Second World War era represents an attempt to address a persistent problem for capitalism, namely its tendency towards overcapacity and over-accumulation – an issue which is particularly acute for the US economy. Driving this process was the need to locate new sites of capital accumulation and new markets for commodities. The search for new sources of accumulation was highly uneven and regionally specific, hardly captured by the market utopianism of the term 'globalization', which entered academic and popular vocabulary after 1990. In the advanced Western and Asian economies, 'globalization' involved an intensification of commodification as new areas of private and public life were colonized by market forces, while many aspects of the Keynesian welfare-state were privatized or downsized. In the former 'communist' countries, the advent of the free market meant the wholesale privatization of state assets and the erection of a kind of gangster-capitalism often abetted by former 'communist' *aparatchiks* and their new allies in Western financial institutions. In the Global South, the imposition of neo-liberalism combined the privatization of state-run enterprises left over from the *dirigisme* of the 1960s and 1970s with a virulent new process of primitive accumulation or 'accumulation through dispossession' (Harvey 2003, 137–182). The latter, propelled by what has come to be called 'financialization', was also one of the main drivers of the 'new imperialism' which emerged during the same period.

In his *A Brief History of Neoliberalism*, David Harvey (2007, 2) defines neo-liberalism as follows:

> Neoliberalism is in the first instance a theory of political economic practices that proposes that human well-being can best be advanced by liberating individual entrepreneurial freedoms and skills within an institutional framework characterized by strong private property rights, free markets, and free trade. The role of the state is to create and preserve an institutional framework appropriate to such practices. The state has to guarantee, for example, the quality and integrity of money. It must also set up those military, defence, police, and legal structures and functions required to secure private property rights and to guarantee by force if need be, the proper functioning of markets. Furthermore, if markets do not exist (in areas such as land, water, education, health care, social security, or environmental pollution) then they must be created, by state action if necessary. But beyond these tasks the state should not venture.

This definition could just as easily serve as a description of the past thirty-five or so years of neo-liberal practices the world over. The vision of the human subject embedded in this definition marks a return to the sort of natural rights individualism that characterized the initial stages of capitalism and a decisive break with the Keynesian state-centred 'national individualism' (O'Connor 1984, 232) of the post-war era. The latter was associated with a pluralistic system of interest group representation (in theory anyway), growing social entitlements and citizenship rights; and rising living standards and consumption levels in most of the advanced capitalist countries. The cultural hegemony of national individualism, which included widespread support for Cold War militarism, rested in the promise that these social and political gains would be protected by an interventionist and activist state. If we were to periodize neo-liberalism in the advanced capitalist world, we can identify at least three distinct phases: the 'shock therapy' of the Thatcher–Reagan years; followed by a second period of consolidation and refinement during the Clinton–Blair administrations in which neo-liberalism attempted to soften its public image through talk of a social economy; and a third way between the market and social democracy and the post-Washington consensus (Fine and Milokanis 2011, 6). To this we may wish to add a third phase, beginning with the 'age of austerity' and sovereign debt crisis following the 2008 financial crisis and ongoing global economic slump. The current regime of privatization, fiscal 'discipline' and turn to authoritarianism unfolding in numerous countries may 'make Thatcher seem like a snatcher of sweets from the pram' (Fine and Milokanis, 7). However we periodize neo-liberalism, one thing is certain; as Neil Smith observes: 'Whatever technical and ideological shifts it implied, neoliberalism brought about a concerted and regressive class redistribution of wealth as the rich got richer and the poor poorer ... neoliberalism was also a quite direct strategy of class struggle' (Smith 2005, 143). Let us turn now to each of these phases.

Margaret Thatcher's (1987) infamous remark (in an interview on 'Aids, education and the year 2000'!) that 'There is no such thing as society' perfectly captures the shift from national individualism to the natural rights individualism of the neo-liberal era. In an earlier part of the same interview, Thatcher (1987) elaborates on her meaning:

> I think we have gone through a period when too many children and people have been given to understand, 'I have a problem, it is the government's job to cope with it!' or 'I have a problem, I will go and get a grant to cope with it!' 'I am homeless, the Government must house me!' and so they are casting their problems on society and who is society? There is no such thing! There are individual men and women and there are families ... and people have got the entitlement too much in mind without the obligations, because there is no such thing as an entitlement unless someone has first met an obligation ...

Thatcher's remarks are really just an echo of the basic tenets of classical liberal thought of the seventeenth and eighteenth centuries. The natural rights individualism developed by the classical liberal theorists assumed that the individual subject is, as it were, an *ex nihilo* creation, already with defined appetites and interests before entering into any organized social arrangements. Not only did this view fit with the Christian view of creation – mankind created out of nothing by God – but also with the 'possessive individualism' of emergent capitalism. The transition from the 'state of nature' to that of 'civil society' might have been a necessity for John Locke, necessary that is for the protection of private property rights, but it was also something of an imposition on our natural disposition to, as Adam Smith would put it a century later, 'truck, barter and trade'. For the classical as well as today's neo-liberals, the 'great and chief end ... of men's uniting into commonwealths and placing themselves under government' as Locke insisted in his *Second Treatise on Government*, 'is the preservation of their property' (Locke 1975, 71). That the property*less* might not see the logic of placing themselves under the rule of such a government or that the state might have obligations beyond protecting the liberties of the propertied did not much trouble the classical liberals.

Thatcher's admonitions against 'entitlements' are in keeping with all of this; her hectoring, moralistic tone betray a fundamental truth about neo-liberal capitalism. As David Harvey observes, the latter required the moralizing ideology of neoconservatism, whether in the form of Thatcher's desire for 'a return to Victorian values' or in the religious idioms of US fundamentalist Christianity, and more recently, in the denunciations of 'deadbeat borrowers': 'Their aim is to counteract the dissolving effect of the chaos of individual interests that neoliberalism typically produces' (Harvey 2007, 83). In other words, the social 'entitlements' and solidarities of the post-war welfare state era needed to be replaced with a new set of expectations. No longer could one speak of a 'right' to housing, employment or health care – all well within the common sense of 'national individualism' – but only of individual rewards of hard work, self-help and familial obligations.

Of course, if moral 'consent' to the new order was not forthcoming, there was always direct coercion. Indeed, the class basis of neo-liberalism is nowhere more apparent than in the way in which it has deployed the law in the interests of property and capital. In 1981, US president Reagan launched his assault on the organized working class by firing twenty thousand air-traffic controllers during the famous PATCO strike. This set the stage for a general assault by employers on the organized working class. In 1983, 20.1 per cent of the US labour force belonged to a trade union. By 2010, this number had fallen to 11.9 per cent of workers (US Bureau of Labor Statistics 2010). As collective bargaining power has declined, so also have real wages. In the US, between 1973 and 2004, real wages fell on average 16 per cent.

Freed from the constraints of union contracts, employers were able to introduce a range of changes to the labour process. Most significant was the introduction of so-called 'lean production' techniques, often involving downsized workforces doing more work at a faster pace due to the introduction of new technologies. Leavened by promises of greater worker control and the use of team work, the reality of lean production turned out to be quite different. As Kim Moody comments: 'From being the "new way of working" that promised a more humane workplace, it has been revealed as a system of brutal work intensification and means of by-passing and undermining unionism' (Moody 1997, 106). Despite rising labour productivity for the sixty million industrial workers of the major Western capitalist countries, workers continue to work forty or more hours per week (the same since 1919) without any decrease in labour-time (Basso 2003, 31).

Greater control over the labour process by employers also translated into an enhanced ability to hire and fire workers more easily or to employ a growing number of part-time and contract workers, thereby bypassing the cost of providing health benefits or pension contributions. Part-time work of up to thirty-five hours per week has been on the rise in all of the developed countries, with a disproportionate impact on women, racialized groups and immigrants. In 2004, the ILO estimated that as a proportion of total employment in most industrialized countries, part-time and contract work increased by one-quarter to one-half over the previous twenty years (ILO, Information Sheet No. WT-4). At the beginning of the economic crisis in 2008, the US economy saw an explosive rise in 'involuntary part-time work' among both young and older workers, increasing by 75 per cent for the latter (US Bureau of Labor Statistics 2008). On a global scale, lean and flexible production ushered in a whole new international division of labour in which outsourcing and just-in-time techniques have had the effect of undercutting 'the power of labor by organizing multiple sources for parts and materials. These multiple sources are not really large factories and nor are they necessarily owned by the central corporate power. Instead, they may constitute a network of quite small and decentralized production locations, even home working' (Smith 2005, 138).

The cumulative effects of these assaults on the working class were profound. It is reckoned that the rate of surplus-value (the ratio of money surplus-value to wages) increased by 40 per cent (Mohun, in McNally 2011, 48). By the late 1980s, the 'shock therapy' phase of neo-liberalism had achieved its primary goal and a new phase of capitalist accumulation had begun: 'The battle had been won. Wages and inflation were tracking down; profits were tracking up … the neoliberal expansion was clearly underway' (McNally, 36). The stage was now also set for 'the financialization of everything' (Harvey 2007, 33). We need to examine this latter aspect of the story more closely.

In August 1971 the Nixon administration, under the guidance of Paul Volker, made the fateful decision to remove its currency from the gold standard which had governed international monetary transactions since the end of the Second World War. From then on, the US dollar – not gold – became the new global currency. Several factors lay behind this decision. First, the costs associated with the war in Vietnam were running up a growing structural deficit. A so-called balance-of-payments crisis was beginning to take hold as creditors began to question the ability of the US to make good its debts in the globally accepted standard of value, namely, gold. Countries holding US dollars in surplus were demanding that payment be made in gold, thus draining away US gold reserves (Gowan 1999, 15–18). At the same time, corporate profitability had been in decline since the mid-1960s. A classic pattern of over-investment in machinery and other means of production during the decades of the post-war boom, had served to undercut the rate of profit. As Marx had predicted, the expulsion of profit-creating surplus labour in favour of machines would result in a falling rate of profit, which is exactly what happened (McNally 2011, 29). Finally, a huge supply of petro-dollars from OPEC countries was flooding into American banks, greatly increasing the money supply which was, in turn, forcing down the value of the dollar. By removing the dollar from the constraints of the gold standard, the US government could let the dollar move as the US Treasury wished. The removal of the gold standard was to have far-reaching consequences, not least as a cornerstone of US imperialism and the 'dollar-Wall Street regime' it established:

> The Nixon administration thus gained its dollar standard and in the upheavals of the early 1970s increasing numbers of countries were forced to abandon attempts to maintain fixed exchange rates between their currencies and the dollar. This suited the US administration because it wished to force revaluation on other states and could now do so through its own policy for the dollar. This was an enormously important development because … the US government could alone among governments, move the exchange price of the dollar, against other currencies by huge amounts without suffering the economic consequences that would face other states which attempted to do the same.
>
> Gowan (1999, 20)

The era of financialization had begun. With the end of the gold standard, money had been unhinged from its anchor in a universally recognized commodity – gold – so that henceforth exchange rates would be allowed to fluctuate wildly. In effect, the value of money was now based on a national credit-money system; individual currencies would be allowed to 'float' against other currencies. This made it increasingly difficult for multinational enterprises to predict the true costs of production or profits since their operation might involve trading in multiple currencies, all of which were now liable to fluctuation on a daily basis. This left only one option: to greatly expand trade and speculation in currencies.

Faced with this new world of exchange rate volatility, investors, banks and speculators rapidly expanded markets that would allow them to buy and sell currencies on an around-the-clock basis. And this explosion in foreign exchange trade only added to the uncertainty, as investors quickly sold off falling currencies while rapidly piling on rising ones. Not surprisingly, currency trading quickly became far and away the world's largest market (McNally 2011, 93).

The turnover in global exchange markets went from a mere $15 billion in 1973 to $3.2 trillion in 2007 (McNally 2011, 93) and became the engine of the exponential rise in the power of finance capital. With so much money floating around in the global system, it wasn't long before financial institutions were looking for ways to lend out money in order to achieve even greater profits. The credit system was about to undergo a massive expansion. And everyone wanted in on the game, even industrial firms which had hitherto left the business of debt and finance to private banks. By 2011, speculative profit-making through financialization topped 50 per cent of the profits of all non-financial corporations (Fine and Milokanis 2011, 6).

If, as we saw previously, money obscures its origins in the productive sphere as a measure of human labour-time, the credit system increases this opacity exponentially. As Marx (1975, 455) was to comment: 'Interest-bearing capital is the consummate *automatic fetish*…money making money, and in this form it no longer bears any trace of its origin.' Interest-bearing capital or credit can take a multiplicity of forms. However, what all of these forms share in common is that they are all forms of what Marx called 'fictitious capital': whether in the form of bank loans, stocks, derivatives and other securities, credit is extended as a future claim on profit. The capital is 'fictitious' because it is merely a promise but not a guarantee of future earnings. It may or it may not produce the expected return on investment. 'Fictitious capital' stands outside production and begins to move to its own laws. It creates 'new instrumentalities and institutions, new class fractions, configurations and alliances and new channels for the circulation of capital itself. All of this is part and parcel of the necessary evolution of capitalism' (Harvey 1999, 327). The growth of 'fictitious capital', like the meteoric rise and fall of stock markets in recent times, *appears* to have taken flight from any association with real values in the sphere of production. 'All connection with the actual expansion process of capital is thus completely lost, and the conception of capital as something with automatic self-expansion properties is thereby strengthened.' The credit system thus takes on 'all manner of insane forms' and is 'transformed into a mere phantom of the imagination' (Marx quoted in Harvey 1999, 269).

Latin America: Laboratory for neo-liberalism

The Volcker Shock, which marked a decisive moment in the global shift towards neo-liberalism, also precipitated a debt crisis which devastated large parts of the Third World and East Central Europe. In so doing, the US had stumbled upon a formula for reasserting its dominance over recalcitrant states in the Global South. As Peter Gowan (1999, 41) observed:

They learned an old truth from the days of European imperialism: the imperial power could take advantage of a country's debt to reorganize its internal social relations of production in such a way as to favour the penetration of its own capitals into that country.

The so-called Baker Plan of 1985, which quickly became known by the euphemism of 'structural adjustment' and policed by the IMF and the World Bank, deployed a simple but consistent formula for debtor nations: removal of restrictions on foreign investment, privatization of public assets, cuts to public expenditures and a reorientation of their economies from 'import substitution' to exports. Servicing their debts meant a massive outflow of funds mainly to US banks. In the 1970s the ratio of debt to total output had been around 7 or 8 per cent. 'Between 1979 and 1987 this ratio went from 16 per cent of output to 39 per cent. Debt payments on interest and principal, which had represented 7 to 8 per cent of exports, suddenly rose to around 23 per cent in 1986' (Dumenil and Levy 2004, 87). Meanwhile, the US and other debt-holding countries of the Global North, by prising open debtor economies, were able to greatly increase their own exports. For the US alone, over half of its exports by the 1990s were to the South, mainly Latin America (Gowan 1999, 71).

So began what Greg Grandin has called 'the third conquest of Latin America', the first being the Spanish conquistadores and the second being the penetration of American corporate power in the nineteenth century (Grandin 2007, 160). Although Grandin has in mind the 'structural adjustment' policies initiated by the Reagan administration, the origins of the new free-market policy of 'trade, not aid' lay further back in time. The original laboratory of neo-liberalism was under the blood-stained dictatorship of Augusto Pinochet in Chile, which overthrew the fledgling socialist regime of Salvador Allende on September 11, 1973. The Pinochet regime, publicly lauded and covertly supported by Western leaders and the business press for stamping out 'communism' in Chile, was an early enthusiast of unbridled free market capitalism. In March 1975, the University of Chicago free market economist Milton Friedman and his 'Chicago Boys' made their first trip to Chile. In his meetings with Pinochet and his advisors, Friedman advocated a 'shock program' in which the further printing of money to finance the state budget was halted, public spending cut by 25 per cent, tens of thousands of government workers laid off, state industries privatized and capital markets deregulated. Some 30 per cent of public enterprises were sold off, often to those with military connections. The immediate effect of the war on inflation and return to the free market was a plummet of GNP by 13 per cent and a collapse of purchasing power by 40 per cent and wages by 20 per cent.

Yet, between 1978 and 1981, the economy expanded by 32 per cent. Ignoring the fact that the economy collapsed again in 1982, the World Bank and the Inter-American Development Bank showered Chile with over forty-six loans between 1976 and 1986, amounting to $3.1 billion (Grandin 2007, 172). Chile and the 'Chicago Boys' attained rock star status among politicians and business leaders who had come to the view that authoritarianism was not necessarily so bad so long as it was deployed in the interests of securing 'economic freedom'. The not so subtle shift towards elevating 'economic' over 'political and social' rights was signalled most forcefully by another University of Chicago economic guru, Friedrich A. Von Hayek, whose 1944 book *The Road to Serfdom*, which had lapsed into obscurity for much of the post-war period, now found avid readers among the general and his advisors.[1] Hayek visited Chile several times, declaring that his 'personal preference ... leans toward a liberal dictatorship rather than toward a democratic government devoid of liberalism' (quoted in Grandin 2006, 173). The Reagan administration had already signalled that as far as it was concerned, the only meaningful human rights were those associated with individual liberty and property rights. As President Ronald Reagan's National Security Advisor Richard Allen put it: 'All too often, we assume that everyone means the same thing by human rights' but for the US it meant strictly 'life, liberty and property' and not 'economic and social rights'. The latter represented a 'dilution and distortion of the original and proper meaning of human rights' (quoted in Grandin 2007, 193–194). Dictatorships, on this view, were perfectly compatible with the protection of 'human rights' so long as these were defined in narrowly economic terms. Thus, the US ambassador to the United Nations under Reagan, Jeane Kirkpatrick, can only have had the Pinochet dictatorship in mind when she formulated her famous distinction between authoritarianism and totalitarian regimes. The former, she argued, could serve the interests of stability and prosperity since they rested on free market principles whereas the latter were associated with the command economies of Soviet empire (Kirkpatrick 1979, 34–45).

Two important pillars of neo-liberal imperialism had thus been forged: a messianic idealism based on the belief that economic freedom was paramount, combined with a foreign policy which was prepared to countenance torture, repression and violent regime change (Grandin 2007, 78). This doctrine, acerbically described by Eduardo Galeano as 'torturing people so prices could be free' (quoted in Grandin 175) would be key to US foreign policy during the 1980s, licensing support for brutal but 'free market' regimes from Apartheid South Africa to El Salvador. But it would also find new iterations closer to our own time in the form of the Bush doctrine of 'preemptive regime change' in the name of 'freedom, democracy and free enterprise' (quoted in Mann 2004, 329) deployed to justify the invasions of Afghanistan and Iraq. The monster first created in the Chilean laboratory has had many lives.

The debt crisis precipitated by Reagan and Volcker's 'shock therapy' quickly spread to other Latin American countries, initiating one of the largest transfers of public wealth into private hands in history. In Bolivia, an orgy of privatizations transferred the state oil company, the telephone system, the national airline, rail system and electric company. When the World Bank ordered the privatization of the water system, the Bolivian government dutifully sold it to the French company, Bechtel. Shortly thereafter, it was announced that water rates would increase by 200 per cent (Grandin 2007, 189). In Argentina, the picture was much the same. The military dictatorship, which came to power in 1976, had taken out massive loans with the blessing of the World Bank and IMF, quietly salting most of the proceeds away in North American banks. Nevertheless, the foreign debt continued to grow, reaching $160 billion by 2001. The same routine of privatizations took place throughout the 1990s, which saw the national airline auctioned off at fire sale prices. It is estimated that in 1990–1992 alone, the Argentine treasury took a $60 billion dollar loss due to privatizations (McNally 2011, 130). Despite this radical surgery, the Argentine economy collapsed in 2002 under the pressure of its foreign debt obligations. As wages and social services were gutted, the number of those living below the poverty line doubled to 58 per cent of the population (Grandin 2006, 201).

Mexico is, in many respects, a case study in neo-liberal structural adjustment when measured in terms of the metrics of race, class, migration and imperial domination. In 1994, under the combined weight of high interest rates on its sovereign debt and a spiralling trade deficit, the Mexican government was forced to devalue the peso. The 'rescue' package brokered by the Clinton administration was really a bailout of US banks and a mechanism through which Mexican billionaires (a new phenomenon) like Carlos Slim Helu were able to further enrich themselves through the purchase of premium public assets such as Mexico's national telephone system. The North American Free Trade Agreement (NAFTA) signed in 1992 linked the Mexican economy to that of the US and Canada. Mexico's privatization programme, which began in earnest in the 1980s, was one of the largest in the world. The number of state-owned enterprises decreased from 1155 in 1982 to 210 in 2003. Meanwhile, union density declined by 25 per cent and real wages by 70 per cent (Roman and Velasco 2011, 248–253). Today, three out of five work in the informal sector.

Along the Mexican-American border, the *maquiladoras* or finishing plants quickly became a major source of cheap labour for large US and Canadian multinationals as well as a magnet for the 1.8 million peasants thrown off their land as a result of the privatization of the *ejido* system of communal land tenure after 1992. Transnational corporations now control nearly every aspect of the food system, from fertilizers to livestock. Harvests of corn and other staples have fallen by nearly 70 per cent for Mexican peasants. As a result the Mexican poverty rate has skyrocketed. A 2011 survey by the main private sector think-tank *El Centro de Estudio Economicos del Sector Privado* (CEESP) determined that 65 per cent of the population lived in some form of privation, and of an active labour force of forty-five million, two-thirds relied on informal employment or other means to survive (*La Jornada*, 21st September 2011). According to another study, the number of people living in poverty amounted to fifty-three million – just over half the population (Roman and Velasco 2011, 249). Meanwhile, 0.3 per cent of the population controls 50 per cent of Mexican wealth (McNally 2011, 129).

Perhaps the most devastating impact has been on women and the indigenous population. Women make up nearly 60 per cent of the Mexican labour force, but half work in the informal sector. As a result, they earn 37 per cent less than male workers. Close to one-third of Mexico's population is indigenous and speak over sixty native languages. The Mayans, Mixtecs, Zapotecs and large sectors of the 'de-indianized' mestizo population, the *mexico profundo* of anthropologist Bonfil Batalla, have suffered the most severe immizeration: 76 per cent are classed as living in extreme poverty. Land dispossession of the peasant and indigenous populations coupled with falling prices due to cheap agricultural imports have been one of the main causes of social conflict in Mexico from the Zapatista Uprising of 1992 to the commune of Oaxaca in 2006 (Cockcroft 2010, 81–91).

From financialization to crisis

By the mid-1990s, a whole new system of international finance and monetary relations was emerging. Now that gold no longer regulated foreign currency transactions, it became increasingly difficult for those conducting business in several different countries to feel secure that the value of the goods and services being traded would maintain their value across different currencies. What if a national currency where they were doing business was to be suddenly devalued, wiping out profits before they could be converted into the currency of their home country? This fear prompted the growth in financial 'risk management' instruments of various sorts. A whole new vocabulary of 'securitization' in the form of hedges, derivatives and credit default swaps gained currency. At its height, securitization 'even created the illusion that risk had disappeared' (Harvey 2011, 17). However, the most important function of these new instruments for managing risk was in the new mechanisms for transferring wealth from those at the bottom of society to those at the top.

Moreover, the theory and practice of 'risk management' and 'securitization' would quickly become a defining ideological trope of the new century, extending its reach far beyond the rarefied heights of Wall Street's bank towers.

The derivative quickly became 'the apotheosis of the new financial regime' (Martin 2007, 31). Although derivatives are supposedly *derived* from the existing value of a commodity, they are in fact more oriented to *future* values:

> Derivatives ... represent a profound transformation in the form of money, in which currencies are no longer linked to past labour (embodied in gold), but largely to future labour, to acts of production and exchange that are as yet unperformed. In this sense, they express a decisive mutation in the form of money in late capitalism.
>
> (McNally 2011, 161)

Derivatives contracts, in other words, can be placed on anything that might be subject to a variation in price. Originating in the need to offset the risks of exchange rate volatility on currency transactions, derivatives trading quickly spread to everything from credit card debt to mortgages and student loans. Debt could now be repackaged as a 'security' and sold on the market. Purchasing credit card debt in the form of a collateralized debt obligation (CDO) could be potentially extremely lucrative, given the traditionally high interest rates on credit cards, yielding gains much higher than stock dividends or bonds (McNally 2011, 99). From the exchange of commodities for money, a whole new market had arisen in which denominated derivative notes could be exchanged with one another in specialized and unregulated 'over the counter' markets (Harvey 2011, 24; Martin 2007, 31). Derivatives markets quickly became a much more popular investment than stocks and bonds. By 2006, $450 trillion in derivatives contracts had been sold compared to the $100 trillion which circulated through global stock and bond markets that year (McNally 2011, 97). By 2008, on the eve of the financial meltdown, the futures market in derivatives and credit swaps reached as high as $600 trillion, including even 'derivatives of insurance contracts on derivatives of asset values' (Harvey 2011, 21). Needless to say, the architects of these exotic hedge funds became famously wealthy, the highest paid fund managers earning $1 billion to $3 billion.

The practice of hedging, placing bets running in both directions against currency exchange rates or interest rates, became the purview of gigantic hedge funds which prowled the world economy looking for gaps between prices in different locations. Placing hedged bets on the future movement of oil, corn, coffee, gold prices, or more recently, on the sovereign debt of entire countries, works in the same way. In 2010, Goldman Sachs created a credit default swap (CDO) which bet that Greece would default on its sovereign debt. Basically a wager on financial collapse, such a hedge makes it much more costly for the Greek government to sell its bonds, thereby increasing the probability of default. As one credit strategist commented, 'It's like buying fire insurance on your neighbor's house – you create an incentive to burn down the house' (*NYT*, 24th February 2010). But that is exactly what is happening. The relatively new market in sovereign debt means that hedge funds which hold such debt win even if they lose. So, for example, the much vaunted 'haircut' which reduced investors' payout on Greek debt in early 2012 triggered payouts of $3 billion to holders of credit default swaps, which meant that actual financial losses were negligible (*Financial Times*, 9th March 2012). Moreover, the deal virtually guaranteed that future payments would be secured by permanently stationing European Union (EU) and IMF banking officials in Athens to oversee the dismantling of pensions, health and social security and public and private sector wage contracts – all to ensure that bankers and hedge fund managers continue to profit.

There was, of course, a built-in incentive in this massive financial structure to keep expanding the circle of debt since it served as the primary engine of financial profit; the idea that banks existed to funnel money into the productive sphere seemed, at best, a quaint relic of a bygone era. Since, now, higher profits could be made through the purchase of derivatives contracts on just about anything, everyone wanted in on the action, from hedge funds servicing the super wealthy, to pension funds, to former industrial giants like General Motors. At one point, General Motors Acceptance Corporation (GMAC) became one of the largest holders of property mortgages and a highly profitable source of auto purchase financing (Harvey 2011, 23). Producing cars became secondary. International Telephone and Telegraph (ITT) resurrected itself as a vendor of small-scale loans or micro-credit to the poor at extortionate rates of interest of between 21 and 30 per cent (Martin 2007, 32). As we shall see in more detail in a moment, profiting from the 'poverty industry' was to reach epidemic proportions in the run up to the crash of the US housing market in 2007–2008.

At the heart of all of this was the increasing amount of banking profits derived from individual and household credit; credit cards, student loans and mortgages; and management fees derived from privatized pension funds. In the face of stagnant or falling real wages since the 1970s, households have become increasingly reliant on credit for basic survival. Between 1980 and 2007, household debt obligations increased from 15.3 to 18.3 per cent of income. As dos Santos (2009, 209) observes:

The class implications have been dramatic. On the one side, we have seen corporate managers and investment-bankers nestled in extensive social and business-networks of capitalist investors and managers, organized professionally with the explicit purpose of maximising returns by shaping market perceptions. On the other side, we have seen atomized individual savers whose engagement with capital-markets is primarily dictated by trying to access consumption – retirement, a child's education, a down-payment on a house, and so on…investment banking during this period appears as monumental and crystallised class-parasitism.

Banks were required by the Basel Accord to hold sufficient capital on their books to offset the risk of their loans, whether these were in the form of banks loans, mortgages or credit card debt. Essentially an elaborate game of pass the potato, banks were enabled to issue mortgages and then sell them off to other financial institutions, which then repackaged them as securities and resold them. The banks were able to charge fees on these transactions but also, crucially, moved the risk associated with the mortgages it sold off its own ledger. The risk belonged to those who purchased the securitized mortgages often bundled together with credit card debt. Banks and financial institutions, therefore, had an incentive to increase the number of loans, credit cards and mortgages they issued and to speed up the trading of securitized debt products since the fees associated with such transactions were highly lucrative. Securitization greatly reduced the risk weighting of loan portfolios since technically the bank no longer 'owned' the loan. This led to a steep rise in the securitization of credit card debt: in 1990, just one per cent of credit card debt was securitized but by 1997, 51 per cent had been. During the same period, Americans charged three times as much as they had a decade earlier (Hyman 2011, 259).

African and Latino Americans, and for a considerable time, women, had long been denied access to credit. However, when it was discovered, for example, that African Americans were three times more likely than the general population to be unable to pay their credit card balances in full on a monthly basis, banks began to flood the market with offers of easy credit. Groups which relied on 'revolving credit', in the main households earning less than $20,000 per year, were also willing to pay higher fees out of necessity to gain access to credit. Moreover, the risk models developed in aid of securitization indicated that there was little risk involved for credit card companies and banks:

Lending to minorities was at the center of the subprime expansion, since this group tended to have no prior relationship with a bank. One-fifth of

Americans had no relationship with a bank, the so-called 'unbanked', and that one-fifth overlapped strongly with the 26 per cent of American households with a credit card. Only 45 per cent of lower-income families had a credit card in 1995. Unbanked Americans were disproportionately African American and Latino. Convincing these groups to apply and then correctly screening them for risk would provide immense profits for the firm clever enough to figure out how to do it.

(Hyman 2011, 270)

With trillions of dollars of securitized financial products circulating in global financial markets, it became extremely difficult for anyone to actually know what they were holding, unless of course, the whole edifice collapsed. But during the feeding frenzy from 2000 onward, the name of the game was to increase the volume of new loans wherever and whenever possible. By 2005, the number of securitized mortgages had increased by 270 per cent (McNally 2011, 102). And 40 per cent of these were 'non-traditional' sub-prime mortgages with escalating interest rates and hidden penalties, sold to poor and unsuspecting purchasers with weak credit histories, mostly to poor African Americans and Latinos, looking to realize the dream of home ownership (McNally 2011, 104). Needless to say, these same groups suffered inordinately from foreclosure once the bubble finally burst in 2007–2008. As one report on the sub-prime mortgage crisis concluded, there existed a deliberate policy of targeting the vulnerable:

More important than all of these consequences is the targeting of people of color and poor people as the best candidates to sign up for one of these loans. In the hands of the mortgage lending industry, subprime loans became predatory loans – a faulty product that was ruthlessly hawked even though financial institutions were aware of its defects. Even a surface check of the demographics shows that, in city after city, a solid majority of subprime loan recipients were people of color ... A deeper look into the crisis reveals that the subprime lending debacle has caused the greatest loss of wealth to people of color in modern US history.

Rivera et al. (2008)

In its moment, the sub-prime crisis lifted the veil from the hidden world of finance capital, revealing just how racist and predatory the regime of indebtedness had become. Tony Paschal, former loan officer for Wells Fargo, reported that some employees referred to the sub-prime loans being peddled to African Americans as 'ghetto loans' for 'mud people' (Barbara Ehrenreich and Dedrick Muhammad, *NYTimes*, 13th September 2009). Since the beginning of the crisis, African American household net worth has shrunk by half and is now twenty times less than the median white household net worth (*Globe and Mail*, 20th April 2011).

However, white working-class and middle-class households have not been spared either. Data from the 2011 US census reveals that one in six, or 46.2 million, Americans now live below the poverty line (*Globe and Mail*, 14th September 2011). Thirty years of wage stagnation meant that for most Americans, the problem was not an increased reliance on credit – credit had always been used to bankroll the 'American dream' – but that they now lacked the ability to pay their debts. The problem, in other words, was structural in nature and not the result of feckless borrowing:

> Instead of seeing extravagant spenders in debt, we should see underpaid workers trying to keep up. Americans personal debt problem resulted not from a choice to borrow but from the rising inequality of income and wealth that had occurred since the 1970s even as capitalist expansion relied on increasing consumption in an era of declining wages. Personal debt was no longer a private choice but a structural imperative.
>
> Hyman (2011, 283)

Even mainstream economists have had to take note. One study published by the Council on Foreign Relations, by Nobel Prize-winning economist Michael Spence and Sandile Hlatshwayo, notes that despite huge increases in productivity or a 21 per cent rise in value-added per US worker, wages and living standards have continued to fall and inequalities to grow. In a study in understatement, Spence concludes, 'One possible response to these trends would be to assert that market outcomes, especially efficient ones, always make everyone better off in the long run…That seems clearly incorrect and is supported by neither theory nor experience' (*Globe and Mail*, 15th April 2011). Markets, it turns out, are extremely efficient engines of social inequality.

The predatory structure of securitization rests on an exponential increase in financial risk. But it was precisely risk and its proper calculation that had become highly profitable. Computer technology was enlisted to speed the circulation of trades such that, for example, the tiniest variations in exchange rates could be executed in micro-seconds. Moreover, tens of thousands of mathematicians and economists, the so-called quantitative experts or 'quants' hired by financial institutions, constructed complex and, as it turned out, fanciful models for minimizing risk and maximizing profit. Mathematical models which married the study of random movements in the physical world with the so-called Efficient Market Hypothesis (EMH) had supposedly solved the problem of pricing risk. Mainstream economics assumes that prices and markets are both rational and efficient. That is, they assume that prices are a reflection of real value and therefore tend towards equilibrium. While this may be true for most commodities embodying measurable quantities of human labour-time, the same does not hold for 'fictitious capital'. Bets taken on anticipated prices may turn out to be, in Marx's words, 'mere phantoms of the imagination'. Even as the crash was unfolding in 2007–2008, the 'quants' insisted that their mathematical models said otherwise (Patterson 2010, 277–278).

Their calculations were based on a model known as Value at Risk (VaR) which operates on the basis of abstract risk such that all forms of risk are reduced to a single variable. The quants devised a formula based on a single number that could be used to gauge if a portfolio was likely to lose money in a twenty-four hour period based on a preceding transaction. If it did, the VaR was adjusted accordingly to signal an increase in risk (Joe Nocera, *New York Times Magazine*, 4th January 2009). What we have is a pricing model for risk in general which can be quantified and therefore, like everything else under capitalism, commodified. So when I purchase a derivative, I am actually purchasing a certain quantity of risk. However, the information yielded by VaR is quite static, since it assumes that prices will remain more or less stable across time; prices one day were likely to be the same the next. Predictions based on such assumptions may rely on data as short as a single business cycle with only slight variations in prices. Even this 'implies a certainty more appropriate to the motions of the heavens. At least astronomers' models have billions of years of data' (Hyman 2011, 279). Time has essentially become ossified:

> Inherent in such models, therefore, is the reification of time, its treatment as a purely quantitative variable. It is as if time is always continuous and repetitive, and qualitative ruptures in the temporal continuum are inconceivable. By deploying reified, mathematical concepts of space and time joined to assumptions of market equilibrium, the models that guided derivative pricing and risk management were doomed to implode the moment a crisis emerged.
>
> (McNally 2011, 111)

And implode they did. Already in 2006, it was evident that the rate of foreclosures among mainly poor African American, immigrant and often single-female led households in older cities like Cleveland and Detroit was skyrocketing. Between 1998 and 2006, such households are estimated to have lost somewhere between $71 and $93 billion in asset values as a direct result of foreclosure on sub-prime mortgages. But, as David Harvey (2011, 1) notes, the mainstream took little notice. If they did, most Wall Street economists predicted that all was well; savvy investors might even profit from a little volatility in mortgage markets. As one oblivious Bear Stearns researcher advised in early 2007: 'While the subprime sector will experience some pain as it removes some of the froth created by excesses...an overreaction to headline risk will create opportunities for nimble investors' (quoted in Patterson 2010, 206). Only in mid-2007, when the foreclosure crisis began to creep into the mainly white middle-class (and Republican) 'sunbelt' states of the US south and west, did questions arise. However, it was already too late.

In June of 2007, *Business Week* reported that the multi-billion-dollar mortgage-backed hedge-fund set up by the Wall Street investment bank Bear Stearns had declined by 23 per cent in less than a year (*BW*, 12th June 2007). The following month, the company announced that its securities were virtually worthless (McNally 2011, 18). The contagion quickly spread, enveloping all of the largest American banks and a number of international lenders as well: in August, France's largest bank, BNP Paribas, froze payments on its mortgage-backed investment funds; in Great Britain, Northern Rock began its decline into bankruptcy. By October, both Citigroup and Merrill Lynch were reporting massive losses in the billions. In March, 2008, Bear Stearns finally collapsed; its shares, trading at $173.00 only a year earlier, now sold for a few dollars. Between July and September 2008, the first act of the financial crisis ended with the collapse of the world's largest mortgage lenders, Freddy Mac and Fannie Mae, with the US government taking over $200 billion in bad debt (McNally 2011, 18).

Act two played out in just under one month in 2008. The collapse of the investment bank Lehman Brothers on 15 September, which wiped out $635 billion in assets, represented the largest bankruptcy in US history. The following day, AIG – the world's largest insurance company – was essentially nationalized by the US government. In quick succession, all of the remaining Wall Street investment banks collapsed: Merrill-Lynch, Citigroup, Goldman Sachs and Morgan Stanley. Later the same month, Washington Mutual fell in the largest bank failure in US history. By now the contagion had become a full-fledged global financial crisis. Banks began to fail in Great Britain, France, Germany, Belgium and Iceland, as governments rushed in to take over their toxic assets. Back in the US, the government poured $25 billion into General Motors and Chrysler to prevent them from going bust (McNally 2011, 20). By the end of the carnage, $35 trillion in global stock holdings had evaporated, as though 'a mere phantom of the imagination'.

The 'automatic fetish' of fictitious capital – 'money making money' – had generated its own 'perfect storm', emboldened by the new pseudo-science of risk management and an equally fetishistic faith in information technology.

This fact was nowhere more perfectly exemplified than by the abject figure of Alan Greenspan, former chairman of the US Federal Reserve, as he testified before Congress in October, 2008:

> In recent decades, a vast risk management and pricing system has evolved combining the best insights of mathematicians and finance experts supported by major advances in computer and communications technology…A Nobel Prize was awarded for the discovery of the pricing model that underpins much of the advance of the derivatives markets…The modern risk management paradigm held sway for decades…The whole intellectual edifice, however, collapsed in the summer of last year.
>
> (quoted in Patterson 2010, 263)

Securitized citizenship

If wage-labour was a formal precondition of citizenship in liberal capitalist societies from the outset, full citizenship in the post-WWII era was also highly dependent on an expanding pool of wage-labour, and crucially, rising wages and profits. The expanding remit of social citizenship rights represented by greater access to post-secondary education, health care and social security was underwritten by the surplus-value produced by the past labours of millions of workers in secure jobs (as well as the unpaid labours of women in the domestic sphere). Here, past labours were a promise of future security. The current crisis has dramatically reversed this temporality: the past is now hostage to an uncertain future. The expectations once inscribed in social citizenship will now be left to the vagaries of financial markets. The chief message for those who continue to cling to the past will be that the wage economy impoverishes (through falling wages and precarious employment) and the market promises: in place of faltering state provision, consumer credit and market-based pensions; private insurance as a substitute for universal health care; student loans in place of affordable tuition and real estate loans in place of social housing; in short, social debts in place of social rights.

The slow accretion of the debt economy into the interstices of social life over the past three decades – what Randy Martin has termed 'the financialization of everyday life' – has brought with it not only a new ethos of self-help and personal dependency on debt and finance to get ahead; it has also connected the fortunes of individual lives to the ebbs and flows of global financial circuits in unprecedented ways. Everyone must now 'think' like a capitalist not only in relation to work but in all spheres of life (Martin 2002).

Finance now moves into the personal; it possesses labor as well as capital, it becomes a practical feature of life – establishing a moral code for the household, integrating it with work, incorporating the future into the present. Effacing the foreign and domestic, finance invites those who can to live by the protocols of risk and those who cannot to accept themselves as beings at risk. At the same time, financialization demands labor for running its apparatuses, whether in the form of investment clubs whose members do their own research, self-help recipes to keep money in motion, or defined-contribution pensions and other schemes that have labor doing the work of finance as well as the work of securing the future which once belonged to the state.

(Martin 2007, 165)

Living with risk, taking risks or being 'at risk' has infiltrated our very definition of the self. As Martin observes, financialization 'insinuates an orientation toward accounting and risk management into all domains of life' (Martin 2007, 43). We are enjoined to think of ourselves as 'human capital', making 'the self a portfolio' (Martin 2007, 187). Individual fortunes are tied to one's entrepreneurial and risk management skills; like fictitious capital itself, our subjectivities are oriented to future rewards in the present:

Today, instead of a consumer-defined middle class, the population is divided into the self-managed and the unmanageable. An articulation of the state with finance, this initiative of rule amounts to a shift away from citizens and consumers and toward investors, and as a new way of framing participation in public life and social policy as a public good. The investor becomes a model for the ideal kind of beings, who manage their affairs and take care of their own future.

(Martin 2007, 8)

Since 2008, these processes have been greatly accelerated through a vast expansion of the debt economy. To pay for the multi-billion dollar bailout of the banking sector, governments have imposed harsh austerity programmes, simultaneously driving down social spending and driving up unemployment. Inequality has spiked as living standards for the majority have fallen. Although the impact of the debt crisis has been uneven, few countries have been spared the rising levels of sovereign debt. According to figures compiled by the Organization for Economic Cooperation and Development (OECD) for the period 2007–2014:

Public Debt as a percent of GDP in OECD countries as a whole went from hovering around 70% throughout the 1990s to almost 110% in 2012. It is now projected to grow to 112% of GDP by 2014 possibly rising higher in the following years. This trend is visible not only in countries with a history of debt problems – such as Japan, Italy, Belgium and Greece – but also in countries where it was relatively low before the crisis – such as the US, UK, France, Portugal and Ireland.

(Cline, Global Finance 2012)

Aggregate figures, of course, disguise the acuteness of the ratios for the most indebted countries. Italy, Ireland and Portugal share debt-to-GDP ratios of close to 130 per cent. And even though both the US and the UK have debt ratios about that of Spain, at 105 per cent, the latter's economic growth prior to 2008 was almost entirely built on over-investment in real estate. Japan with a ratio of 230 per cent has been mired in slow growth for many years owing, in part, to its eclipse as an industrial power by China. Nevertheless, it retains a substantial industrial base when compared to Greece with a debt-to-GDP ratio of 200 per cent.

More than anywhere, Greece has become the new laboratory of neo-liberal austerity. The 240 billion euro bailout Greece has received under the tutelage of the IMF, the European Central Bank (ECB) and the European Commission (EC) has entailed steep cuts in public sector spending and employment and a massive programme of privatization of state assets. Since 2009, the economy has contracted by 20 per cent with a loss of approximately 1000 private sector jobs per day. An additional 300,000 public sector jobs have been deliberately eliminated, with another 75,000 to disappear by 2015. With cuts to pensions, health care and education, the Greek government has slashed social expenditures by 43 per cent in five years (Reguly 2013).

Globally, around 200 million people are officially considered unemployed according to the ILO, a figure expected to continue to rise past 2017. Twenty-eight million jobs have been lost since 2008. Moreover, thirty-nine million have dropped out of the labour market, opening a job gap of sixty-seven million jobs since 2007 (ILO 2013). Growing youth unemployment has now reached catastrophic proportions in the Eurozone. In the zone as a whole it sits at 25 per cent but in Southern Europe is much higher: in Italy it has reached 40 per cent; in Spain it has reached 60 per cent; and in Greece it is expected to top 70 per cent in early 2014 (Thompson 2013). Rarely reported in the financial pages is the human cost of prolonged unemployment. In Greece, between 2007 and 2009, before the worst cuts had yet taken hold, the male suicide rate increased by 24 per cent, in Ireland by 16 per cent and in Italy by 52 per cent. In Spain, numerous press reports have appeared chronicling the suicides of individuals about to lose their homes due to foreclosure (Povoledo and Carvajal 2012).

In the US, although official unemployment is considerably lower than in Europe, the human effects of the crisis have been profound owing to a much thinner social safety net prior to the crisis. US census data for 2010 reports that while one in six live below the official poverty line, another 104 million Americans or nearly one-third of the population are below twice the poverty line. For a family of three that means an annual income of $38,000 (Edelman 2012). A Federal Reserve study in 2012 found that between 2007 and 2010 the average family lost 39 per cent of its wealth (*Globe and Mail* 2012). Even at that, white incomes are still 20 times greater than those of African Americans. Between 2005 and 2009, net worth of the median household among African Americans fell by over 50 per cent to a pathetic $5677 (Yakabuski 2011).

On the other side of the class ledger, however, the economic crisis has been a boon for the wealthy. As economists Piketty and Saez have shown, the share of income of the top 1 per cent in the US has been growing steadily since the beginning of the neo-liberal revolution. Between 2002 and 2007, it shot up to nearly 62 per cent of all income compared to 6.8 per cent for the 99 per cent (Saez 2013). Since 2008, 93 per cent of income gains went to the richest 1 per cent while the super-rich, who comprise one-tenth of the top 1 per cent, have gained two-thirds of the total (Reich 2012). These would be the same people who received $700 billion in bailout money from the US Treasury in 2008–2009 under the Troubled Asset Relief Program (TARP). Only recently revealed, however, is the fact that the US Federal Reserve secretly funnelled an astonishing $7.7 trillion to the financial sector, most of which went to the six biggest banks (Morgenson 2011). For the 99 per cent, incomes increased by a derisory 0.2 per cent (Freeland 2012). As Oxfam (2014) revealed, we now live in a world in which the 85 richest individuals control as much wealth as the poorest half of the global population – 3.5 billion people.

'All roads to the future', Richard Deinst (2011, 27) observes, 'lead through an immense pile of debt.' Debt has become one of the chief engines of neo-liberal accumulation and dispossession, 'a machine for capturing and preying on surplus-value' (Lazzarato 2012, 21). It has also become the pretext for remaking whatever remains of the tattered bonds of liberal citizenship, 'a kind of reverse image of contemporary solidarity' (Deinst 2011, 56). 'Consent', once a cornerstone of liberal democracy, begins to lose much of its meaning, or rather to have its meaning recast as the 'obligation' to pay one's debts. In doing so, it returns the very idea of citizenship to its origins in the commodity form, in the supposed equal exchange between appropriators and producers:

Perhaps the notion of 'consent' makes more sense when it is pronounced 'obligation', deflecting the subjective orientation from the political realm (with its vestigial symbolic rituals, parties, etc.) to the economic realm where it signifies a prior agreement to abide by the rules of exchange.

(Deinst 2011, 77)

How else are we to interpret the Eurogroup's praise for the Greek government's agreement to rewrite its constitution in order to guarantee that banker's interests are given priority over those of citizens? In a 2012 statement they write: 'Finally, the Eurogroup in this context welcomes the intention of the Greek authorities to introduce over the next two months in the Greek legal framework a provision ensuring that priority is granted to debt servicing payments. This provision will be introduced in the Greek constitution as soon as possible' (Eurogroup Statement 2012). Or, to take another example, consider Mario Monti's appointment as Italy's unelected prime minister in November 2011. Rising yields on government bonds, it was decided, took precedence over elections as Monti quickly introduced draconian austerity measures which cut pensions, raised taxes and reformed the labour code so that workers could be fired more easily.

In order to recast the bonds of citizenship, as Marx long ago recognized, it is also vital to remake the self. In some of his earliest reflections on the role of money and credit in social life, Marx had this to say:

Credit is the economic judgment on the morality of a man. In credit, the man himself, instead of metal or paper, has become the mediator of exchange, not however as a man, but as the mode of existence of capital and interest. The medium of exchange, therefore, has certainly returned out of its material form and been put back in man, but only because man himself has been put outside himself and has himself assumed a material form. Within the credit relationship, it is not the case that money is transcended in man, but that man himself has turned into money, or money is incorporated into him. Human individuality, human morality itself, has become both an object of commerce and the material in which money exists. Instead of money, or paper, it is my own personal existence, my flesh and blood, my social virtue and importance, which constitutes the material, corporeal form of the spirit of money. Credit no longer resolves the value of money into money but into human flesh and the human heart. Such is the extent to which all progress and all inconsistencies within a false system are extreme retrogression and the extreme consequences of vileness.

(Marx 1844, 6)

Marx is at pains in these passages to show that far from returning social relations to a more humane basis in personal trust as some socialists at the time thought, the creditor–debtor relationship is based on just the opposite. For Marx, the credit system was nothing short of a vast apparatus for deepening and extending the alienation of labour under capitalism. By colonizing the bonds of mutual trust, the credit system inserts itself into the very fibres of individual morality and subjectivity. As a supplement to the ideology of hard work and self-sacrifice in the productive sphere, the indebted worker now becomes 'the *mediator* of exchange … as the *mode of existence of capital*' thus completing the circle in which the abstract labours of the worker return in the spectral form of debt to feed from within on the 'human flesh and the human heart'. Debt plays a disciplinary role as the guilt associated with indebtedness is internalized and individualized; the debtor is inveighed with accusations of feckless spending or, more recently, 'deadbeat' borrowing. In so doing, debt shifts the focus from social causes to personal failings and from universal remedies to individual solutions. The debt economy thus becomes one of the main drivers for the dismantling of social rights in favour of individual responsibility and obligation (Lazzarato 2012, 131).[2]

The dialectic between longer working hours and the self-work of the indebted now form two sides of a single coin. While falling real wages have been the primary cause of indebtedness, finding and keeping paid employment, however precarious, has also eroded the divide between working time and non-working time. While it is widely acknowledged that working hours (including work done outside the workplace) have increased by 20 to 30 per cent over the past three decades, it is seldom recognized how much personal time is devoted to the self-work required to get or retain employment. As Boltanski and Chiappello note, for many groups of workers in the advanced capitalist world, the original liberal idea of self-ownership has reached its ultimate expression in the 'labour of self-fashioning' whether in the form of online profiles, fashion or bodily fitness. Under 'the new spirit of capitalism' they write:

> the distinction between private life and professional life tends to diminish under the impact of a dual confusion: on the one hand, between qualities of the person and the properties of their labour-power … and on the other, between personal ownership and, above all else, self-ownership and social property lodged in the organization. It then becomes difficult to make a distinction between the time of private life and the time of professional life, between dinners with friends and business lunches, between affective bonds and useful relationships, and so on.
>
> (Boltanski and Chiapello 2005, 155)

The erosion of the division between work-time and private life, Boltanski and Chiappello argue, is the result of a more thoroughgoing restructuring of capitalism over the past thirty years. The shift from bureaucratic to more self-activated forms of control was part of a concerted effort by employer groups to co-opt elements of what they term the *artistic* critique of capitalism which emerged out of the social movements of the 1960s. The artistic or cultural critique emphasized the lack of individual autonomy, creativity and feelings as against the instrumental reason and bureaucratic rationality governing large institutions from the university to the industrial firm. The artistic critique was, above all, about the *values* and *processes* which governed such institutions: alienation, authoritarianism, oppressive attitudes towards women and racialized minorities and in the workplace, Taylorism, lack of autonomy and the separation between the conceptual and manual aspects of work. Running alongside the artistic critique in the 1960s was a more fundamental *social* critique of capitalism, which emphasized issues of class inequality, exploitation and social security. The combined effects of neo-liberal restructuring and the exhaustion of many of the class-based movements in the late 1970s meant that the social critique of capitalism was sidelined in favour of the anti-bureaucratic struggle for autonomy (Boltanski and Chiapello 2005, 178). This situation provided an opening in which it became possible for employers to substitute a new ethos of *self-control* and personal autonomy for older methods of external, top-down control. By appearing to cede ground to the cultural critique while turning it to its own purposes, capitalism was able to escape the constraints of the social critique and open the way to more *flexible* forms of exploitation in the workplace and greater social inequality (Boltanski and Chiapello 2005, 199).

In the new world of contingent and precarious labour, which characterizes many professional and semi-professional fields such as information technology, advertising, the service industry, cultural production, and increasingly, post-secondary education, affective labour and flexibility have become the new markers of success:

> [T]he qualities that are guarantees of success in this new spirit – autonomy, spontaneity, rhisomorphous capacity, multitasking (in contrast to narrow specialization of the old division of labour), conviviality, openness to others and novelty, availability, creativity, visionary intuition, sensitivity to differences, listening to lived experience and receptiveness to a whole range of experiences, being attracted to informality and the search for interpersonal contacts – these are taken directly from the repertoire of May 1968…and placed in the service of forces whose destruction they were intended to hasten.
>
> (Boltanski and Chiapello 2005, 97)

As with the creditor–debtor relationship, in the flexible workplace, the bonds of mutual trust are exploited as a means of self-control. The worker is intended to internalize a morality of trustworthiness and dependability as a prerequisite of team work and 'networked' forms of labour. Trust, usually associated with personal relationships, has been colonized as a form of market behaviour conducive to financial success: 'an internalized belief in the sincerity of the bond established for a certain length of time – while presenting the continual establishment of new connections as a prerequisite of profit creation' (Boltanski and Chiapello 2005, 457).

The ethos of self-control and illusion of autonomy have been greatly abetted by the spread of information technology. Mobile and 'smart' devices have allowed for new forms of horizontal control and self-management which extend far beyond the workplace. The labour of self-management through interaction with digital devices now monopolizes an astonishing amount of time, seamlessly linking self-work, paid employment and consumption.[3] As Jonathan Crary (2013, 72) observes, 'we may not grasp that to decline this endless work is not an option'. The myriad forms of self-fashioning and self-control now available through digital technology are at one with the forms of class power associated with financialization and the future-oriented moral economy of debt. The immersion and externalization of the self within digital formats, however interactive, is ultimately a form of reification closely aligned with processes of commodification and financialization (Crary 2013, 99). Whether in the form of the self-work involved in finding or maintaining paid employment, retiring debt or consumption, the digital imprint of our lives is now subject to endless data mining by corporations, credit agencies, and, as is now obvious, by the security state.

Across the global system, over thirty years of neo-liberal restructuring, culminating in the post-2008 economy of debt and austerity, has dramatically reshaped both subjective expectations about future security as well as the formal character of citizenship – from social rights to social debts. To these terms must be added another: a security state whose unchecked powers of surveillance have fed upon a disabling politics of fear.

Notes

1   The latest 'rediscovery' of von Hayek is by Tea Party supporters who helped push *The Road to Serfdom* to the top of amazon.com's bestseller list in 2010.
2   As Margaret Atwood notes in her book, *Payback: Debt and the Shadow Side of Wealth*, debt is now counted as one of the cardinal sins:

> There are even debt TV shows, which have a familiar religious-revival ring to them. There are accounts of shopaholic binges during which you don't know what came over you and everything was a blur, with

tearful confessions by those who've spent themselves into quivering insomniac jellies of hopeless indebtedness, and have resorted to lying, cheating, stealing and kiting cheques between bank accounts as a result. There are testimonials by families and loved ones whose lives have been destroyed by the debtor's harmful behavior. There are compassionate but severe admonitions by the television host, who here plays the part of priest or revivalist. There's a moment of seeing the light, followed by repentance and a promise never to do it again. There's a penance imposed – *snip, snip* go the scissors on the credit cards – followed by a strict curb-on-spending regimen; and finally, if all goes well, debts are paid down, the sins are forgiven, absolution is granted, and a new day dawns, in which a sadder but more solvent man you rise the morrow morn.

(quoted in Graeber 2011, 378)

3   A 2010 Nielsen survey showed that daily consumption of televisual content for the average American amounted to five hours per day (Crary 2013, 84).

3

'Securitizing' Empire: Small Wars and Humanitarian Fantasies

Theorizing imperialism

In Chapter 1, we explored the origins of the liberal subject and how we might begin to theorize citizenship under capitalism using the tools provided by Marx's critique of the commodity form. Now, we need to examine more closely the relationship between the basic dynamics of capitalism and imperialism. For, while it is true that contemporary capitalism still cleaves to its original ideal of a propertyless legal subject, it is important to stress that historical development has often deviated from this norm. Capitalism, as we have seen, has not developed in a particularly uniform fashion, owing in large part to the particular configuration of class forces and the trajectory of class struggle over time in different societies and cultures. The history of capitalism, as David Harvey (2011, 155) has urged, is a history of 'seemingly chaotic forms of uneven geographical development'. One reason for this is that capital accumulation always seeks to overcome geographic boundaries, something already glimpsed by Marx and Engels (1972, 63–65) in a justly famous passage of the *Communist Manifesto*:

> The need of a constantly expanding market for its products chases the bourgeoisie over the entire surface of the globe. It must nestle everywhere, settle everywhere, establish connections everywhere … It compels all nations on pain of extinction to adopt the bourgeois mode of production; it compels them to introduce what it calls civilization into their midst, i.e., to become bourgeois themselves. In a word, it creates a world in its own image.

In the *Grundrisse*, Marx (1973, 408) comments that 'the *world* market is directly given in the concept of capital itself. Every limit appears as barrier to be overcome'. Some have insisted that such passages prove that Marx saw the incorporation of the non-capitalist world into capitalism as a more or less linear and inevitable process. However, while he may have believed that capitalism would eventually triumph over all non-capitalist social forms, he was also keenly aware that the spread of capitalism was a far from peaceful or linear affair. Simply because capital strives to overcome every barrier to its expansion, 'it does not by any means follow that it has *really* overcome it'. For two reasons: first, the 'universality towards which it irresistibly strives encounters barriers in its own nature' in the form of crises generated by its own inherent contradictions, and second, because those whom it seeks to subjugate to the ruthless logic of primitive accumulation often resist and disrupt the rule of capital. Moreover, as Marx (1973, 414) observes in the same passages of the *Grundrisse*, capitalism has never been a homogenous system of exploitation with a single unitary centre but a competitive system comprised of 'many capitals':

> Conceptually, competition is nothing other than the inner nature of capital, its essential character, appearing in and realized as the reciprocal interaction of many capitals with one another, the inner tendency as external necessity. Capital exists and can only exist as many capitals, and its self-determination therefore appears as their reciprocal interaction with one another.

For Marx, in other words, capitalism was characterized by a systemic compulsion to constantly expand profits in the face of rival capitalists grouped within a system of competing nation-states. Competitive accumulation means that individual capitalists, whether they like it or not, are locked into a system which compels them to constantly reinvest and expand their operations. They can, of course, choose to simply hoard their profits, but to do so, as Marx (1977, 254) remarks, means that they have ceased being a capitalist and merely become a miser. In order to remain competitive, capital must expand its spatial operations at the same time as it reduces the temporal distance between locations. Marx (1973, 539) referred to this as the tendency to 'annihilate space through time'.

Capitalism can be understood as a circuit of spatial and temporal movements where an individual capitalist starts with a given quantity of money, M, which is exchanged for commodities necessary for production, C, which include labour power, Lp, and raw materials and machinery, Mp. All of these elements are combined in production, P, to produce a new commodity, C' and a profit or increase in the initial monetary investment, M'. This circuit can thus be expressed:

$$M.....C.....P (Lp + Mp).....C'.....M'$$

The capitalist circulation process requires that more and more aspects of social and natural life across the planet be subjected to its logic. That means turning as many people and things as possible into commodities which can be bought and sold on the market for a profit. In more technical terms, it involves transforming the qualitatively diverse use-values which are needed to sustain human life into exchange-values, the quantitative equivalent of money. Capitalism is constantly attempting to expand the range and nature of things which can be commodified; from hand soap to health care, from land to leisure time and from human affect to the human genome, all have been colonized by the relentless expansion of the commodity form. At the same time, the geographic reach of capital now encompasses virtually the entire planet. In short, the drive to expand and intensify capitalism's command of the social and natural life-world is an in-built structural feature of the system. As Adam Hanieh (2006, 178) summarizes:

> The logic of the circuit can thus be summarized in four basic themes: (1) maximizing the sphere of activities encompassed by capitalist social relations; (2) maintenance of a system of private property rights; (3) minimizing any restrictions or barriers to the flow of capital; and (4) the role of the capitalist state as the guarantor of capitalist social relations.

In *Capital*, Volume One, Marx explicates the 'vertical' relationship between wage-labour and capital, while leaving until Volume Three, the 'horizontal' relations between 'many capitals' and their implications for capitalist economic crises. Further volumes were planned, on wage-labour, the state, international trade, the world market and crises, but remained unwritten in Marx's lifetime (Marx 1977, 28). A fully realized theory of imperialism, as Alex Callinicos (2009, 79) has argued, must take account of both the 'vertical' and 'horizontal' aspects of the capitalist circulation process. Two points are worth stressing here. First, as we saw in Chapter 1, the 'vertical' relations between capital and wage-labour are founded on the historic separation of the economic and the political such that political power is devolved to the separate sphere of the state. This does not mean that all actually existing capitalist states underwent the same process of separation or that states do not play a central role in many economies. It means rather that capitalism (unlike pre-capitalist societies which rested on the application of 'extra-economic' forms of political power in order to appropriate an economic surplus from the direct producers) has fashioned a unique system of *market coercion* rooted in 'the historical process of divorcing the producer from the means of production'. Market coercion means that the indirect and impersonal compulsions of the market – the worker's need to sell his or her labour for a wage or go hungry – is a distinctive and historically far more effective form of labour exploitation than any which have preceded it. From a capitalist point of view, market coercion, due to its impersonal and relatively disguised nature, is much more reliable and less fractious than politically charged forms of surplus-extraction. Secondly, however, because capitalism is comprised of diverse and unevenly developed national centres of capital accumulation locked in competition with one another, capitalism has historically relied on a system of nation-states to police the interests of these various nationally based capitals. Capitalism did not invent the existing state system but rather inherited it from feudal society. The multiple state system 'is the result of the historical fact that it emerged against the background of multiple feudal states, and, in the course of its development transformed the component states of that system into capitalist states but failed to alter the multi-state character of the resulting international system' (Brenner 2006, 84). As Ellen Wood (2003, 139) has observed:

> the state lies at the very heart of the new global system... the state continues to play its essential role in creating and maintaining the conditions of capital accumulation; and no other institution, no transnational agency, has even begun to replace the nation state as an administrative and coercive guarantor of social order, property relations, stability or contractual predictability, or any of the other basic conditions required by capital in its everyday life.

An earlier generation of Marxist theorists had already grasped that capitalism had indeed given rise to a global imperialist system based on the two dimensions outlined above: a 'vertical' system of exploitation based on the capital relation and a 'horizontal' system of competing nation-states. To this extent, they correctly grasped that mature capitalism is inevitably imperialist; the outward push of capital, its search for new geographical sources of accumulation, is an inbuilt feature of the system. Secondly, they recognized that the existence of 'many capitals' embedded within a plural system of nation-states tended towards – though didn't necessarily always result in – armed conflict. These were the basic premises of Lenin and Bukharin's attempt to theorize capitalist imperialism in the early decades of the last century. Bukharin's (1972, 107) insight was that the creation of a world economy through the 'internationalization' of capital was at one with 'nationalization' of capital, the tendency of individual capitalists to more closely integrate themselves with their national states:

> The development of world capitalism leads, on the one hand, to an internationalization of the economic life and, on the other, to the levelling of economic differences, – and to an infinitely greater degree, the same process of economic development intensifies the tendency to 'nationalize' capitalist interests, to form narrow 'national' groups armed to the teeth and ready to hurl themselves at one another at any moment.

As perceptive as this analysis was in light of the military rivalries which sparked the First World War, it still remains that state activity is seen as a reflex of national capitals as they seek out new markets, raw materials and cheap labour. To pose the relationship between the exploitation of wage-labour and capital and the state-system in this way has always been deployed by Marxism's critics as an example of economic reductionism. We need then to look more closely at how the current generation of theorists have dealt with this problem.

The new imperialism

Contemporary Marxists have sought to distance themselves from the reductive implications of Bukharin's formulation by positing a dual logic approach in which states and capital are dialectically linked but not reducible to one another. Alex Callinicos (2009, 74) challenges the 'Lenin-Bukharin synthesis' by arguing for a theory based on 'two logics of power, capitalistic and territorial, or two forms of competition, economic and geopolitical'. This formulation is largely in agreement with David Harvey's (2003, 183) contention that:

> Imperialism of the capitalist sort arises out of a dialectical relation between territorial and capitalist logics of power. The two logics are distinctive and in no way reducible to each other, but they are tightly interwoven. They may be construed as internal relations of each other. But outcomes can vary substantially over space and time. Each logic throws up contradictions that have to be contained by the other.

Harvey (2003, 137–182) argues that although neither process is reducible to the other, capitalism's territorial expansion is inextricably linked to what he terms 'accumulation by dispossession'. Accumulation by dispossession derives from Marx's analysis of 'original' or 'primitive accumulation'. In chapter 26 of Volume One of *Capital*, Marx (1977, 875–876) famously describes the basic social relation required for capitalism to come into being:

> The capital-relation presupposes a complete separation between the workers and the ownership of the conditions for the realization of their labour. As soon as capitalist production stands on its own feet, it not only maintains this separation, but reproduces it on a constantly expanding scale. The process, therefore, which creates the capital-relation can be nothing other than the process which divorces the worker from ownership of the conditions of his own labour; it is a process which operates two transformations, whereby the social means of subsistence and production are turned into capital, and the immediate producers are turned into wage-labourers. So called primitive accumulation, therefore, is nothing else than the historical process of divorcing the producer from the means of production. It appears 'primitive' because it forms the pre-history of capital, and of the mode of production corresponding to capital.

As we saw in Chapter 1, this definition of primitive accumulation does indeed describe a real historical process, especially the consolidation of English capitalism in the seventeenth and eighteenth centuries. However, it is important to stress that it only imperfectly describes the transition to capitalism in other European states as well as other parts of the global system where capitalism was in the process of expanding its operations through the aegis of colonial domination. Historically speaking, capitalism has been quite promiscuous in its ability to coexist with and eventually conquer a variety of forms of surplus-extraction from slavery to handicraft and small-scale peasant production. The reason Marx occasionally used the term 'capitalist slavery' to describe the plantation system in the Caribbean and southern US was because of a distinction he drew between the *formal* and *real* subsumption of labour to capital. As Marx (1977, 1021) observed, the *formal subsumption* of labour to capital may involve taking over 'an *existing labour process*, developed by different and more archaic modes of production'. By contrast, the *real subsumption* of labour to capital, what Marx terms 'the specifically capitalist mode of production', involves the complete dispossession of the direct producers and their transformation into market dependent wage-labourers. While it is undoubtedly true that, at the level of *total* social capital, free wage-labour is essential, at the level of the individual capitalist enterprise, both free and unfree forms of labour are capable of contributing to the accumulation of surplus-value (Banaji 2010, 142–143).

But, it is also important to understand what we mean by the term *free wage-labour*. First of all, to assume that labour is 'free' in the sense that it is allowed to circulate in the labour market, therefore making it un-coerced, is mistaken. Indeed, *all* forms of wage-labour, even those based on a free labour contract, are to some degree coerced:

> ... *all* wage-labour is subject to compulsion, both in the general and widely accepted sense that workers are compelled to sell their labour-power and subject, at this level, to a general market or economic coercion, and more directly, insofar as the exchange involved in wage-labour is one of 'obedience for wages'; and employers have to find ways to enforce contracts. Given that all wage-labour is subject to constraint in this double sense, it follows that the 'freedom' of free labour is best construed in a *minimalist* sense to mean, *primarily*, the legal capacity ('autonomy') required to enter a labour agreement.
>
> Banaji (2010, 150–151)

Wage-labour, therefore, spans a variety of labour forms, from more or less coerced to more or less free forms of wage-labour. Indeed, for much of the world's working population today, wage-work in the 'formal' sector is often combined with work in the 'informal sector'; the latter may be for wages, often far below the standard minimum wage and often sporadic, or it may take the form of street-vending, home production or provision of services (McNally 2011, 225). Dispossession, not a 'free' labour contract, is what is important for capitalist accumulation. So, while 'accumulation by dispossession' today is undoubtedly rooted in the logic of capital accumulation, a combination of 'archaic' and 'specifically capitalist' labour forms and processes may coexist, depending on historical conditions. The imposition of 'structural adjustment' on the countries of the Global South has produced a rate of urbanization fuelled by migration from the countryside to cities in which fully 80 per cent of the urban population in the least-developed countries live in slums heavily reliant on informal and semi-formal labour in order to survive (Davis 2007, 23). Even in China, which in many ways followed a classic path of 'proletarianization' as millions of dispossessed peasants were drawn into urban factories, many workers still return to their villages to grow food at certain times of the year.

All of this has implications for how we think about the subjects of contemporary imperialism and the kind of citizenship rights which are likely to emerge in its wake. The teleology of liberal political and legal theory (and much of development economics) would have us believe that with the development of market capitalism, democratic rights and processes are likely to follow. A central reason for this has to do with the fact that liberal theory associates free labour with the autonomous subject of liberal citizenship. However, liberal contract theory has 'sanitized wage-labour in the sanguine images of individual autonomy, private volition, free will and agency' (Banaji 2010, 131). This was the point of Marx's denunciation of the 'mystifications' and 'illusions about freedom' which obscured the real unfreedom of the wage relation and which, as I earlier argued, forms the basis of the fetishistic form of the 'citizenship illusion'. The uneven and combined nature of the labour forms we find in those regions most affected by imperialism (and even those less affected, like China) means that linear accounts which see free wage-labour as a precursor of some illusory ideal of liberal citizenship are unwarranted.

Quite the opposite is the case: since the beginning of the neo-liberal era, informal and semi-formal labour has grown exponentially. In Latin America, four out of five new jobs have been in the informal sector, and in Africa it is estimated that close to 90 per cent of new employment will be in the informal sector (Davis 2007, 176–177). The vast majority of these workers do not enjoy even the most minimal economic rights, let alone anything resembling social citizenship rights. Nor is it likely that the informal sector is simply a way station on the road to formal employment. The wider impact of informalization is often felt most acutely by the most economically vulnerable: 'increasing competition within the informal sector depletes social capital and dissolves self-help networks and solidarities essential to the survival of the very poor ... especially women and children' (Davis 2006, 184). And, because survival often depends on individual competition, this situation can produce an 'enclosed self' immune to the bonds of reciprocity and community solidarity (McNally 2011, 225). However complex the mix of informal and formal work may be for some workers in the Global South, the vast majority will be condemned to the Hobbesian hell of informal labour. If it is possible to locate an 'ideal' imperial subject, it is surely here.

Today, 'accumulation by dispossession' encompasses the myriad ways capitalism has developed to separate the direct producers from control over the means of subsistence:

These include the commodification and privatization of land and the forceful expulsion of peasant populations; the conversion of various forms of property rights (common, collective, state, etc.) into exclusive private property rights; the suppression of rights to the commons; the commodification of labour power and the suppression of alternative (indigenous) forms of production and consumption; colonial, neo-colonial, and imperial processes of appropriation of assets (including natural resources); the slave trade and usury, the national debt, and ultimately the credit system as radical means of primitive accumulation.

Harvey (2007, 145)

Harvey and Callinicos's 'two logics' approach has the advantage of not reducing imperialist rivalry between states or groups of states as always directly involving economic interest as well as allowing for the vagaries of political and military decision-making in different contexts. This is an important point, provided that the 'internal relation' between economics and politics is not jettisoned in the process. To do otherwise would be to fall into the neo-Weberian trap – made famous by Theda Skocpol (1979) – of assigning *completely* separate logics to the state and capital. The 'dual logics' position appears at times to want to place the territorial expansion of the state on a par with the extra-territorial dynamic of capital accumulation. However, as Robert Brenner has observed,

... the logic of territorial states lacks a *raison d'etre* and there seems little empirical warrant for it. Compare the near-permanence of the borders of the main capitalist states over centuries with the impermanence of capitalist firms, even the greatest of them...The bottom line is that it is difficult to specify an actual social force based in the state that possesses interests in conflict with those of capital in terms of foreign policy.

Brenner (2006, 81–82)

It is more sensible, therefore, as attested by Harvey's (2011, 204) later formulation, to speak of a nexus of relations linking the extra-territorial logic of capital accumulation and the territorial logic of the nation-state. Throughout the history of capitalism, the latter has served as the key mediator and manager of the place-based political, cultural and institutional traditions. These include variants of nationalism and militarism and crucially, the imprint left on the state by democratic and anti-democratic movements.

The close alliance of state power with corporate and financial interests highlights an important feature of contemporary imperialism. Far from being of declining importance as argued by some early theorists of 'globalization', the state has become much more the naked servant of neo-liberal capitalism, even at the cost of shedding some of its former powers of social legitimation. 'Public policy' has become more and more the polite expression for furthering the interests of capital. The imperial state today deploys it economic, political and cultural resources to buttress and secure the interests of capital. Especially in times of crisis, the state is called upon to bail out capitalists, secure banking assets and work tirelessly to insure that the fragile international financial system does not collapse. Meanwhile, international financial institutions like the IMF, the World Bank, the International Development Bank (IDB) and the World Trade Organization (WTO) have become allies and surrogates for the imperial states in the extension of capitalist interests and social relations throughout the world (Petras and Veltmeyer 2005, 35–51). Even the United Nations, through its Millennium Development Goals, has become a vehicle for a new imperialist project of spreading capitalism to the developing world (Cammack 2006). This is not to deny that the relationship between the state and capital and supra-national organizations is complicated by the emergence of regional blocs such as the EU, the North American Free Trade Agreement (NAFTA), the Central American Free Trade Agreement (CAFTA), Mercosur and informal currency agreements between China and other Asian countries. As Harvey (2007, 67) has argued,

> capitalism now works within a hierarchy of scales that are not necessarily easily co-ordinated … the state … now nestles within a newly constructed hierarchy of institutional arrangements that have much to do with how the 'new' imperialism is being constructed … the state may be fundamental but its sovereign powers have changed along with the range over which state effects are felt.

This highlights a danger of viewing the new imperialism as emanating from a single centre or nation-state. While the deployment of US military might is the most attention-grabbing aspect of the new imperialism, imperialist rivalry *between* states and economic blocs is just as important, even if such competition remains for a time latent. Imperialist rivalry is the product of *systemic* imperatives resulting from competitive accumulation between different units of capital within a plural states system. The fact that no single nation-state or group of states, however powerful, can police the entire global economy means that military power and warfare will remain a key feature of the imperial system. And when terrorist violence beyond the state is thrown into the mix, the problem becomes even more intractable. As Ellen Wood (Empire 2003, 144) has argued, a more or less *permanent* state of warfare – war without end – has become definitive of twenty-first century capitalism: 'Boundless domination of the world economy, and of the multiple states that administer it, requires military action without end, in purpose or time.' Moreover, although economic competition for investment, markets, resources and cheap labour have not yet generated the kind of military conflicts which characterized earlier phases of imperialism, it is not unreasonable to assume that with the ascendancy of new capitalist powers such as China, Russia and India such conflicts will emerge in the future. We should expect that at some point China will exhaust its internal sources of capital accumulation and begin to systematically seek out 'spatial fixes' elsewhere with the inevitable ratcheting up of inter-imperialist rivalries. Indeed, the recent 'strategic pivot' of US military resources towards the Asia-Pacific and away from regions like the Middle East is indicative of the emerging military might of China.[1] So, while America is the pre-eminent military power and still has the largest economy on the planet, its superiority in firepower vastly exceeds its economic supremacy. It is this imbalance between its economic and its military might which helps account for the shift to a more aggressive military posture. Thus, the drive of the second Bush administration towards a more coercive orientation in international relations was intended to send a message not only to so-called 'rogue' regimes and 'failed' states, but also to its major economic competitors. Geopolitical competition between states, although not reducible to economic imperatives, has a great deal to do with securing the best possible conditions of capital accumulation for its national and regionally based capitals.

There are, of course, significant differences between older forms of colonialism and contemporary imperialism. Territorial domination, though not entirely absent, is not the main *modus operandi* of the new imperialism. The latter is fundamentally about the attempt to implant capitalist social-property relations across the planet; it is about the universalization of capitalism as a social and political system. Notwithstanding its own history of internal colonization (and near annihilation) of Native Americans, in the modern period, the US has been able cloak its imperial ambitions in the language of anti-imperialism. Unlike the older European imperial states, America never had a formal territorial empire based on the military and political subordination of its colonies. By the twentieth century, most of its earlier experiments in building a territorial empire were abandoned not because it thought better of it, but quite simply because it had no choice: the world had already been carved up by other colonizing states (Smith 2005, 48). For example, the British Empire, at its height, encompassed nearly one-third of the globe and was based on an elaborate system of economic and political domination overseen by a system of career colonial administrators from the home country and willing collaborators drawn (and sometimes artificially created) out of the ranks of the native population. As the European empires fell into crisis after the First World War, the US was able to present itself to the world as an opponent of colonialism and a defender of the right of less powerful states to self-determination. This had little to do with any superior moral code of conduct in international affairs and everything to do with its largely unrivalled economic power. America could dominate the world, as the great architect of liberal imperialism Woodrow Wilson quickly recognized, not through the construction of a territorial colonial empire but through the informal empire of the market. As Neil Smith (2005, 70) has observed:

> Put bluntly, the traditional strategy of geopolitical power and control was blocked for US capitalists ... Instead of controlling the flow of raw materials and finished products with all the expense of customs, factory legislation, a civil service, and a military presence across the globe (in addition to the capital investment itself), US capital would refocus on controlling the flow of productive and finance capital into and out of sectors and places that could remain technically independent – self-determining – but that would, by dint of US economic power, be controlled for all intents and purposes, by US interests.

So, the interest in the doctrine of self-determination and the spread of liberal ideals had largely to do with the ascendency of a new 'globalism' and the push for 'openness' of the world market to the products of American capitalism. One of the great advantages of informal empire is that the US has been able to 'conceal its imperial ambition in an abstract universalism ... to deny the significance of territory and geography altogether in the articulation of imperial power' (Harvey 2003, 50). That is why Barack Obama can so confidently declare that 'we stand not for empire, but for self-determination' (*Washington Times,* 22nd June 2011).

However, the ideology of 'openness' and the implied universalism of market globalism were central to the articulation of US nationalism at home. America has always seen itself as a 'beacon on the hill', stretching back to the time of its first Puritan settlers embodying universal values of freedom, democracy and the sanctity of private property. From the Monroe Doctrine which sanctioned US hegemony over Latin America in the name of anti-colonialism to the doctrine of Manifest Destiny which justified the colonization of Native lands in the western US; from *Time* magazine publisher Henry Luce's call for 'a new American century' at the beginning of the Second World War to make the world safe for democracy to the contemporary neoconservative architects of the invasion of Iraq, the Project for a New American Century (PNAC), American nationalism has always been closely allied to a global, ostensibly universalist, mission:

> Whereas the geographical language of empires suggests a malleable politics – empires rise and fall and are open to challenge – the 'American Century' suggests an inevitable destiny. In Luce's language, any political quibble about American dominance was precluded. How does one challenge a century? US global dominance was presented as the natural

result of civilization, rather than the competitive outcome of political-economic power. It followed as surely as one century after another. Insofar as it was beyond geography, the American Century was beyond empire and beyond reproof.

Smith, quoted in Harvey (2003, 51)

Risk management warfare: From Vietnam to Iraq

This was only ever a partial truth. Indeed, the history of America's relations with smaller states has much more often been characterized by the deployment of military might in the interests of market 'openness' than it has been by the vaunted respect for the right of self-determination. For example, while grandly proclaiming the doctrine of national self-determination, Woodrow Wilson was sending troops in to Haiti, Nicaragua, Mexico and the Dominican Republic (Retort and Boal 2005, 86). Nor did he have any patience for Native American or African American experiments in self-determination (Smith 2005, 80). Coercion, rather than persuasion, has tended to be the weapon of choice for dealing with recalcitrant populations at home and abroad. Small, regionally based wars or interventions, often employing the services of pliant local elites, have been the preferred method for policing American economic interests, which, as one recent champion of such conflicts confesses, 'might as well be called imperial wars' (Boot 2002, xvii). Approximately sixty such 'small wars' were fought or sponsored by the US across the twentieth century. In the post-Second World War period alone, the list of military interventions is staggering. The implementation of National Security Council Report 68 (NSC-68) in 1950 set the stage for aggressive military interventions wherever it was felt that US interests were threatened by rival states. Invasions, incursions or coups were sponsored in Iran (1953); Lebanon (1958); South East Asia (1958–1960); Indonesia (1965); Africa (1965–1966); and Lebanon (1982–1983) (Retort 2005, 88). In Latin America, which Greg Grandin (2007) has rightly termed 'empire's workshop', coups or proxy-wars were initiated in Guatemala (1954); Ecuador, Guatemala and Honduras (1963); Brazil and Bolivia (1964); the Dominican Republic (1965); Chile (1973); Nicaragua in the 1970s and 1980s; El Salvador (1980s); Grenada (1983); Panama (1989); Venezuela (2002); Haiti (2004); Honduras (2009); and Paraguay (2012).

The danger of 'small wars' of empire is that they can turn into major ones, resulting in the perennial danger of 'imperial overreach' as happened most spectacularly for the US in Vietnam. American defeat at the hands of the Vietnamese famously established the conditions for the 'Vietnam

Syndrome' – the belief that America could not and should not fight wars it could not guarantee it would win. And winning in military terms meant the deployment of overwhelming force, preferably against much weaker enemies, as in the Grenada or Panama invasions. The same guiding principle was in force in the 1991 Gulf War. It may have been premature for George Bush Sr. to declare an end to the Vietnam Syndrome after that conflict since the very small number of allied deaths had not yet sufficiently tested the American public's willingness to accept a larger number of casualties. The 'Vietnam Syndrome' proved alive and well in the aftermath of the Somalian debacle of 1993 where 1200 US troops were routed by local warlords and forced to withdraw. The 'Clinton Doctrine' which dominated military policy for the rest of the 1990s sought to avoid American casualties at all cost. Economic 'openness', now enshrined under the equally euphemistic ideology of 'globalization', would be secured by means of 'a modern equivalent of old-fashioned "gunboats" in cruise missiles and aircraft armed with precision-guided munitions' (Bacevich 2002, 148).

Clinton-era 'globalization', backed by the occasional salvo of cruise missiles or NATO-sponsored bombing campaigns, appeared to be all that was required to maintain American hegemony. Indeed, state-military power seemed to recede into the background. Under the Clinton administration, the National Economic Council was more powerful than the National Security Council, and the Treasury and the IMF became the principle instruments of American foreign policy (Mann 2004, xvi). The hidden hand of the market combined with 'soft' and largely invisible policy intervention seemed to herald a new era of what the president of Microsoft liked to call 'frictionless capitalism' (Gates 1995). Liberal globalists, postmodernists and Madison Avenue advertising gurus alike, were seduced by capitalism's apparent ability to morph into a benign engine of cultural flows, hybrid identities and consumer empowerment. Moreover, those most mesmerized by globalization tended to mistake neo-liberal downsizing of the welfare state for its wholesale decline. Fluid flows of finance capital aided by new communications technologies had made the old state order itself redundant and the world safe for a 'kinder and gentler' form of capitalism. Or so it seemed.

In the 1990s, neoconservative intellectuals had become increasingly preoccupied with the role of state military power both in the war on terror but also more broadly in the protection of American imperial interests. In the 1990s, Francis Fukuyama trumpeted the 'end of history' doctrine which held that liberal capitalism had vanquished all other contending ideologies; all that the 'hidden hand' of the market required to work its benign magic was the minimalist 'night watchman' state beloved of classical liberal theory. Lately, he has begun to question the wisdom of unbridled neo-liberalism, arguing for a reassertion of the '*techne* of state-building' (Fukuyama 2004, 99). 'For the 9/11 period', Fukuyama (2004, 120) writes, 'the chief issue for global politics will not be how to cut back on stateness but how to build it up ... the withering away of the state is not a prelude to utopia but to disaster.' In a similar vein, Philip Bobbit (2003, xxi) links the emergence of what he calls, in a strikingly apt term, 'the market-state' to American victory in the epochal wars of the twentieth century. The system of nation-states, and the right to self-determination upon which the concept of national sovereignty rested, has come to an end. In future, state legitimacy will rest less on welfare or democratic principles and more on its ability to secure purely market-based rewards for its citizens. But the market itself is incapable of coordinating the defensive tactics required to guarantee these outcomes. The role of the 'market-state' is precisely to deploy sufficient military might such that challenges to market-based societies are forestalled. Robert Kagan (2003, 3) echoes these sentiments, arguing against what he takes to be the European delusion that the world has entered a 'post-historical paradise of peace and relative prosperity, the realization of Immanuel Kant's "perpetual peace"'. Rather, 'the United States remains mired in history, exercising power in an anarchic Hobbesian world where international rules and laws are unreliable, and where true security and the defense and promotion of the liberal order still depends on the possession of military might' (Kagan 2003, 3). It is easy to see the fit between such cavalier dismissals of the supposed encumbrances of 'old-fashioned' notions of state sovereignty and the right to self-determination – if these can ever be said to have been an obstacle for imperial states – and the Bush doctrine of 'preemptive war'.

In an important sense, the idea of 'the market state' was the natural adjunct of the thinking which underlay the so-called Revolution in Military Affairs (RMA) which was seen as a means through which small wars could be kept small (Metz and Kievit 1995). Its main purpose was to avoid the catastrophe of another Vietnam by minimizing American casualties through the deployment of maximum force. RMA doctrine was steeped in the same fetishistic obsession with information as that found in the financial sector: quantification, informatics, cybernetics and surveillance; a reduction of all risk factors to an abstract quantum stripped of qualitative value – a calculus as content in the war room as it would later be on Wall Street. Indeed, as Randy Martin (2007) has argued, the triangulation of the neo-liberal 'market state', the risk management calculus of finance capital and the new war doctrine cultivated by both Democratic and Republican administrations was not an accidental occurrence. If it is possible to identify an 'imperial unconscious' (Martin 2007, 126), it is surely expressed in the intersection of these three terms. The RMA contains within it a risk calculus not unlike that employed by financial 'quants' who attempt to reduce all qualitative threats to a single quantitative value; like financial derivatives, the doctrine of pre-emption attempts to anticipate future terrorist threats by bringing them into the present on the basis of an abstract calculus of risk. This logic of 'inevitable futures' was even embodied for a brief period in a Pentagon programme, Policy Analysis Market (PAM), which established a 'terrorist futures market' in which 'players' would provide intelligence similar to insider trading markets. As Elmer and Opel (2006, 486–487) observe:

> In short, the program would allow on-line, real time betting on the likelihood of the next terrorist attack…The Policy Analysis Market was based on the efficient market hypothesis, the central premise being that collective thought, and in particular insider knowledge, is more accurate than individual opinion or policy analysis from a distance…In a contradictory and somewhat confusing attempt to harness the power of market incentive while limiting potential profit from terror and manipulate the markets, bets were to be limited to $100. This price cap was also said to be a way to minimize the cost to the government as they expected to lose money to well informed investors.

Although the 'terrorist futures market' was abandoned by the Pentagon after an uproar in Congress, its basic logic remained emblematic of the new risk management strategy signalled by the RMA and the new theory of 'small wars'. *Joint Vision 2020*, released in 2000, with its famous declaration of 'full spectrum dominance' was also a study in the use of limited but high-tech deployment of military resources. In the hands of Defense Secretary Rumsfeld it meant a leaner military which used mobility, stealth and precision to deploy the greatest force while minimizing the risk of military casualties. It was, above all, a strategy to make armed conflict 'a low-risk enterprise' (Bacevich 2010, 162). As Randy Martin (2007, 101–102) argues, the ethereal world of financial securitization had spawned its own terrible twin in the form of 'derivative wars' of empire:

> Derivative. Securitization. Risk. How might these keywords of finance be seen as the fruits of battle? Our small wars of late have been tied to big ideas. A highly interventionist privatizing state. Deliberately restricted applications of resources intended to be leveraged to larger effects. The breakup of fixed values, the dispossession of populations from their productive capacities in search of new opportunities…Military intervention for liberation would become the means and end of politics, and force would become the kind of change agent once reserved for the idea of development. Aid would

remain a promise, forever falling short of expectations. While positioned to go anywhere, intervention would remain highly selective, hoping that a couple of well-placed calls might ripple throughout the world. All this under the sign of evangelical capitalism.

Iraq would become the laboratory in which the new imperial formula was tested: the tactics of risk management warfare would become the catalyst and stabilizing agent for a *sui generis* market state on the banks of the Tigris. 'Military neoliberalism … (the) radical, punitive, "extra-economic" restructuring of the conditions for expanded profitability' (Retort 2005, 72) had become, quite literally, the order of the day. In early 2003, Paul Bremer, the American appointed pro-consul proudly declared, 'It's a full-scale economic overhaul … We're going to create the first real free market economy in the Arab world' (quoted in Doran 2012, 144). With shameless haste, Bremer proceeded to privatize 200 firms while cutting the corporate tax rate from roughly 45 per cent to a flat 15 per cent. Investors were also allowed to take 100 per cent of their profits out of the country. Order 39 insured that any investor who feels that their profits are threatened by Iraqi government actions can sue in a third-party international dispute settlement court (Klein 2007, 415). The privatization of national assets under an occupying force is illegal under international law. Reminded of this fact, one contractor reportedly replied: 'I don't give a shit about international law. I made a commitment to the President that I'd privatize Iraq's businesses' (quoted in Doran 2012, 151).

Nor apparently did the UN Security Council care much for international law, since it granted the Coalition Provisional Authority full control of the Development Fund for Iraq, overseen by a board comprised of representatives from the World Bank, IMF and the UN. With the blessing of the high priests of neo-liberalism, the looting of Iraq was allowed to continue apace. Such complicity by international institutions is less an example of how powerful states are prepared to ignore international law in pursuit of their imperial interests than it is an illustration of how far the latter has become integrated into the imperial system. The post-facto legal rationalization of the deployment of imperial power has a long pedigree in international affairs; what is new, as Danilo Zolo (2009, xii) argues, is

… the victors' justice applied to vanquished, weak and oppressed peoples, with the collusion of international institutions, the acquiescence of the majority of academic jurists, the complicity of the mass media and the opportunistic support of a growing number of self-proclaimed 'non-governmental organizations', which are at the service of their governments' interests.

Meanwhile, in the political sphere, the new constitution was engineered to prevent any future Iraqi government from reversing the new rights granted to capital. Constitution Act 26, promulgated in 2005, renders the Bremer orders inviolable while CPA Order 96 established a party political system based on sectarian ethnic and religious lines. In effect, sectarianism was being constitutionalized (Doran 2012, 14). As one UN official commented after the 2005 elections, 'The election was not an election but a referendum on ethnic and religious identity' (quoted in Hersh 2005). In fact, most Iraqis were opposed to sectarian federalism:

> Contrary to the impression purveyed by the media, federalism is opposed by a clear majority of Iraqis – by a majority of Sunnis and a majority of Shiites alike. According to a July 2005 survey conducted by the International Republican Institute, a US government-funded entity tasked to build the machinery of pro-free market Iraqi political parties, 69 percent of Iraqis from across the country want the constitution to establish 'a strong central government' and only 22 percent want it to give 'significant powers to regional governments'. Even in Shiite-majority areas in the south, only 25 percent want federalism while 66 percent reject it.
>
> Seymour (2012, 225)

Though the US tried, and ultimately failed, to forestall the transition to democratic rule, they were on balance able to guarantee that whatever party or sect ultimately controlled the reins of power, the state would remain securely tethered to a market economy. In practical terms, this has involved the crafting of forms of civic life which insure capitalist hegemony through both subjective and structural means through the creation of real but extremely limited forms of democratic participation and citizenship while at the same time instituting a regime of private property rights behind a *cordon sanitaire* of legal protections impermeable to popular control. One commentator has aptly labelled this 'an ideological process that should be rightfully referred to as "democratism", the acceptable face of authoritarian rule' (Ali 2001). At its core, this involves embedding a system of substantive class rule alongside formally democratic political and civic institutions. In other words, it involves the creation of a system of capitalist social-property relations in which political and economic relations are confined as far as possible to separate spheres.

For good measure, the CPA made sure that the elimination of the bulk of Iraq's $120 billion debt was firmly tied to a 'structural adjustment' programme overseen by the IMF. Two conditions were fundamental: elimination of government oil subsidies for the domestic market and a new oil law that would set out the legal framework for private investment in the sector. As Christopher Doran (2012, 165–166) observes:

> In dealing with a new Iraq, liberated from the oppression of Saddam Hussein, Iraqis would be subjected to the exact same neoliberal market treatment the US and First World has forced on the rest of the planet. Whether the occupation and troops remain doesn't matter in the long run; what matters is putting in place mechanisms to ensure Iraq becomes and remains a neoliberal American-dependent client state.

The patrimonial state which has emerged from the US occupation was born of blood, torture and systematic terror; in this context parliamentary democracy was little more than a facade. The June 2004 promulgation of Frago 242 (Fragmentary Order 242) which instructed troops not to investigate breaches of the laws of armed conflict opened a floodgate: from the routine use of torture at Abu Ghraib to the slaughter in Fallujah in November, 2004, – which almost certainly involved the criminal use of white phosphorus by coalition troops – reveal how entrenched and mundane such barbarities had become. The so-called 'Salvador Option' – first deployed in Central America in the 1980s – was a counter-insurgency strategy based on the use of death squads targeting anyone perceived as being sympathetic to the Iraqi resistance. Championed by General David Petraeus and created by its original architects, former Honduran ambassador John Negraponte and Colonel James Steele, the Special Police Commandos (SPC) set up in September, 2004, were intended to staunch the growing, largely Sunni-led insurgency. However, as Peter Maass (2005), who first reported on the strategy, concluded: 'In El Salvador, Honduras, Peru, Turkey, Algeria, and other crucibles of insurgency and counterinsurgency, the battles went on and on. They were, without exception, dirty wars.'

As the Iraq war disappears down the memory hole of American popular consciousness, its outcome has by no means been an unalloyed success for the 'risk management' warfare of contemporary imperialism. The stated reasons for the war, 'to disarm Iraq of weapons of mass destruction, to end Saddam Hussein's support for terrorism and bring freedom to the Iraqi people' (Bush 2003) were never more than a thinly veiled propaganda exercise, despite being championed by numerous intellectual apologists from across the political spectrum (Mooers 2006). The non-existence of 'weapons of mass destruction' and Saddam Hussein's non-support of Al Qaeda terrorists have become emblematic of government mendacity and media credulity. The counter-insurgency strategy championed by the US military, from Donald Rumsfeld to General David Petraeus, can hardly be seen as the 'risk management' success the Revolution in Military Affairs promised it would be. About all that can be said for ten years of war and occupation is that the US managed to avoid the kind of traumatic defeat it had experienced in Vietnam. The much-vaunted military 'surge' at the end of the Bush administration was, as Andrew J. Bacevich (2013, 20) has argued, only capable of 'staunching the bleeding', not of delivering victory:

> Future historians may well classify the surge as a myth concocted to perpetuate a fraud. The myth centers on the claim that a strategy devised in Washington and implemented by a brilliant general saved the day. The fraud is that a 20-year military effort to determine the fate of Iraq yielded something approximating a positive outcome.

As for bringing 'freedom to the Iraqi people', the sectarian nature of the Iraqi state has come fully into view: Shiite, Sunni and Kurds remain deeply divided, with open civil war now a reality. Moreover, the current regime supports the Syrian government in the civil war and is a close ally of Iran. A 2013 study by Brown University's 'Costs of War Project' observes that terrorism in the region has greatly increased as a result of the invasion. The study conservatively estimates 190,000 Iraqi deaths directly attributable to the US-led invasion, 70 per cent of them civilians. US combat deaths in Iraq were relatively slight at 4487, compared to the Vietnam War which saw 58,000 US deaths and lasted nearly twice as long. However, with over 32,000 wounded, the rising cost of veterans' care is expected to add $1.7 trillion to the total cost of the Iraq war, which is estimated to top $3.9 trillion by 2053. Meanwhile, the health care infrastructure of Iraq, once one of the best in the region, remains devastated by sanctions and war as half of the country's medical doctors fled the country over the past decade. The $60 billion supposedly spent on reconstruction of infrastructure such as roads, hospitals and water treatment facilities largely went instead to the military and the police apparatus (Watson Institute for International Studies). As for 'bringing freedom to the Iraqi people', the record is clearer: 'Violence and torture have been the hallmarks of the US in Iraq, not democracy and the rule of law' (Doran 2012, 239).

The early exuberance that 'the first free market economy in the Arab world' would open up Iraqi oil fields to US control turned out not to be the case. In 2007, the Iraqi Parliament, with the help of US advisors, began to secretly draft legislation towards a new oil law. The new law would have allowed foreign oil companies to develop Iraq's fifty non-producing oil fields for up to thirty years with guaranteed contracts prohibiting changes to the terms of the contract, even if the price of oil drastically increased. Most importantly, the law contained a provision that insured that investor-state disputes would be referred to a third-party arbitration tribunal which could overrule Iraqi courts. Only the concerted efforts of the Iraqi Federation of Oil Workers (IFOU) and other civil society organizations prevented this neo-liberal dream law from being implemented (Doran 2012, 168–172). Ironically, it has been China, and not the US, which has gained the greatest access to Iraqi oil fields, buying half the oil Iraq now produces. As Michael Makovsky, a former State Department official during the Bush administration observed in 2013, 'We lost out. The Chinese had nothing to do with the war, but from an economic standpoint they are benefiting from it, and our Fifth Fleet and air forces are helping to assure their supply' (Arango and Kraus 2013).

Does this mean that 'military neoliberalism' was a failure? Doran makes the case that Iraq was a success when judged against the broader goal of expanding free market neo-liberalism in the region. First, whoever assumes governmental power in Iraq, the 'market state' fashioned by the US, binds the Iraqi people to the dictates of the IMF, the WTO and the World Bank. Second, the Iraq invasion demonstrated US commitment to ensuring military security for its allies in the region, Israel and the states which comprise the Gulf Cooperation Council (Bahrain, Kuwait, Oman, Qatar, Saudi Arabia and the United Arab Emirates), as well as advancing the cause of the US-Middle East Free Trade Area (MEFTA) in the region (Doran 2012, 177–182). The Gulf Cooperation Council (GCC) states have in recent years become a significant centre of indigenous capital accumulation – *khaleeji-capital* – centred on oil and gas but including an increasingly integrated web of construction, real estate, commercial and financial enterprises. And unlike Iraq and Iran, which must rely on their domestic working classes to fuel development and therefore remain vulnerable to the kind of challenge mounted by Iraqi oil workers, the GCC states have used migrant labour drawn from outside the region, lacking even the minimal protections of citizenship.[2]

The Obama doctrine: Afghanistan and beyond

It is a sad irony that millions of Americans believed that the devastation inflicted by the Bush regime and its allies in Afghanistan and Iraq was somehow an aberration and that under Barack Obama the US would return to a more benign foreign policy. There is, of course, some truth to the claim that the turn towards a more aggressive foreign policy in the aftermath of the attacks of 9/11 and the willingness to use 'preemptive' military force to achieve its goals did represent a significant policy shift. Different administrations do indeed pursue different policy agendas. But, as argued above, to see such developments in purely ideological and policy terms both exaggerates the level of choice involved and underestimates the historic continuities of US foreign policy. As one of the conservative apologists for US foreign policy, including the invasions of Afghanistan and Iraq, contends, America 'is an empire that dare not speak its name. It is an empire in denial' (Ferguson 2004, 317). On foreign policy issues, therefore, the Obama presidency should be seen as part of a continuum and not, as some have supposed, as a fundamental break from the imperialist policies of the past. As Ross Douthat observed in the *New York Times*, the 'Obama Doctrine' simply means 'Fewer boots on the ground, but lots of drones in the air. Assassination, yes; nation-building no. An imperial presidency with a less-imperial footprint' (Douthat 2013). In certain respects, because of his supposed liberal credentials – a fact recognized by many conservatives – Obama has been given much more of a free ride than his predecessor (Bergen 2012; Barker 2013). As Tariq Ali (2011, 37) has observed, the contrast between the supposedly aberrant Bush regime and that of Barack Obama was from the beginning ripe for myth-making:

> In reaction, the election to the presidency of a mixed race Democrat who vowed to heal America's wounds at home and restore its reputation abroad was greeted with a wave of ideological euphoria not seen since the days of Kennedy. Once again, America could show its true face – purposeful but peaceful; firm but generous; humane, respectful, multicultural – to the world… Rarely has self-interested mythology – or well-meaning gullibility – been more quickly exposed. There was no fundamental break in foreign policy, as opposed to diplomatic mood music, between the Bush One, Clinton and Bush Two administrations; there has been none between the Bush and Obama regimes.

In Afghanistan, Obama has largely continued the previous administration's counter-insurgency campaign, even adopting the 'surge' strategy pioneered in Iraq by deploying an extra 30,000 troops in 2009. Despite the isolation of the Afghan resistance, it now seems clear that Afghanistan will end for Obama much as Iraq did for George W. Bush, with no decisive military victory and little to show for over ten years of war. The Karzai regime cannot even claim a patina of democratic legitimacy. Election corruption was so widespread in 2010 that the US momentarily denounced the outcome, only to later congratulate President Karzai on his victory (Ali 2011, 60). Without US and NATO support, it seems almost certain that the regime would not last very long. The final proof of the regime's tenuous hold on power came when Karzai shamelessly admitted that tens of millions of dollars had been delivered to his office in order to buy the support of regional warlords deeply involved in the drug trade; his only worry seemed to be that with all of the publicity about 'ghost money', the CIA might consider cutting the payments off. When he met with the CIA station chief, he reported, 'I told him because of all these rumors in the media, please do not cut all this money, because we really need it' (Rosenburg 2013).

While Afghanistan does not represent the type of economic prize that the Iraqi oilfields represented, the US has tried to ensure that neo-liberal economic reforms are given a foothold. In 2010, the State Department optimistically reported that Afghanistan 'has taken significant steps toward fostering a business-friendly environment for both foreign and domestic investment' such as providing foreign ownership guarantees (Skinner 2010, 3). To be sure, there are known reserves of lithium and copper as well as the possibility of a gas pipeline from resource-rich Central Asian states. But, the reasons for the war in Afghanistan were far more geopolitical than they were straightforwardly economic. The pretext for the invasion was, of course, payback to the Taliban regime for harbouring Al Qaeda. But the larger context was the establishment of a military bridge-head against the fast rising powers of China, Russia and India (Skinner 2010, 9).

Despite these considerations, there is a curious way in which Afghanistan fits within the economic logic of the new imperialism. The evident reliance of the Karzai regime on the largesse of CIA cash payments highlights how such patrimonial regimes become tied to global circuits of money capital, very little of which ever finds its way into productive investment. Alex de Waal (2010, 40) has commented with great insight on the 'dollarization' of conflict:

> With economic liberalization and the growth of informal and international criminal economies, and above all with economic globalization, convertible currency drives out all other currencies, monetary and non-monetary, in which loyalty can be bought and sold. Material reward is at the centre of the patronage system, but in the last generation patronage has become not only monetized but 'dollarized'. Political markets, no longer confined to a single country, are now joining up across borders and becoming global. Symbolic rewards such as titles and ribbons are valued less – cash is what counts.

Indeed, 'dollarized' proxy wars are emerging as a key component of the latest phase of the 'risk management warfare' being pursued by the Obama administration. With the counter-insurgency strategy now in tatters in the wake of Iraq and Afghanistan, the 'Obama Doctrine' now sees proxy armies as a way of avoiding US casualties while prosecuting the newest frontiers in the global 'war on terror'. Africa, for example, is becoming 'the prime location for the development of proxy warfare, American style' (Turse 2012, 73). Not surprisingly, proxy warfare has been central to the Pentagon's 'pivot' towards the Asia-Pacific region with 'partnerships' being forged and joint military exercises held with India, Australia, Indonesia, Malaysia, New Zealand, the Philippines, Singapore, South Korea and Thailand. But a monetized 'proxy' strategy has the greatest appeal for the most impoverished nations. Pursuing a strategy uncannily similar to the derivatives-backed mortgage schemes which targeted poor African Americans, the proxy wars of the future look to exploit the same desperation when it comes to pursuing US military hegemony:

> These proxies-in-training are, not surprisingly, some of the poorest nations in their respective regions, if not the entire planet. They include Benin, Ethiopia, Malawi, and Togo in Africa, Nepal and Pakistan in Asia and Guatemala, Nicaragua and Honduras in the Americas.
>
> Turse (2012, 77)

As noted above, a second major cornerstone of Obama's 'risk management' military strategy involves the growing use of the unmanned killing machines known as drones. In an important sense, this represents the acme of 'securitized' warfare: like some distant derivative trader seeking to leverage a small trade to maximum effect, the 'pilot' who decides to rain hellfire missiles down on unsuspecting victims in Libya, Pakistan, Yemen or Somalia, is likely sitting at a remote-control console somewhere in the Nevada desert or one of over a thousand other US bases worldwide.

Obama has ordered over 300 drone strikes compared to fifty under George W. Bush. The number of drones in use has increased exponentially since 2003 from 50 to over 7500 such that the US Air Force now trains more remote pilots than it does fighter or bomber pilots (Benjamin 2012, 87). Only when Republican Senator Lindsey Graham enthusiastically revealed in a speech to Rotarians that drone strikes had killed over 4700 people did the Obama administration feel compelled to justify its strategy. All sources agree that only about fifty of these deaths represent 'high value' Al Qaeda and Taliban targets.[3] In other words, the vast majority were either civilians or what the CIA calls 'low level' insurgents, which appears to be a determination based on where people are living. Citizenship, in this instance, counts for nothing; four US citizens who were deemed to represent 'an imminent threat of violent attack' have also been killed in drone attacks. The elasticity of the term 'imminent threat' and the high number of civilians killed in so-called 'double-tap' strikes where rescuers are killed by a second strike after having rushed to the aid of those killed by the first, led UN special rapporteur Christopher Heyns to declare such strikes *war crimes* (Serle 2012).

Nevertheless, illusions about Obama's supposed liberal credentials still prevail: 'cant still goes a long way for those who yearn for it' (Ali 2011, 73). While liberal Democrats would likely have decried the drone policy had it been pursued by a Republican president, Obama has largely silenced them. As Joan Walsh discovered, the number of white 'racial-liberals' (those with progressive views on race) supporting the use of drones nearly doubled from 27 per cent to 48 per cent when told that president Obama favoured such a policy (Walsh 2013). This suggests that liberal presidents like Clinton and Obama are much more effective than their conservative counterparts at winning the hearts and minds of the American electorate when it comes to prosecuting imperial strategy. Having surrounded himself during his second term with prominent 'liberal interventionists' such as Susan Rice and Samantha Power, some are predicting a new golden age for 'humanitarian interventions' of the kind practiced in Libya.[4] While George W. Bush won over many liberal intellectuals to the war camp in the run up to the invasion of Iraq, others remained wary. Now, their man has his hand on the wheel.

'Humanitarian' imperialism

In the past decade, 'humanitarian intervention' has added an important new ideological dimension to the politics of informal empire. Leavening the tactics of 'military neoliberalism' was a new doctrine of human rights which had taken root during the long consolidation of neo-liberal hegemony. The culture of privatization inaugurated during the Reagan-Thatcher era sanctioned an explosion of 'a multiplicity of "sovereign free actors" worldwide' (Weizman 2011, 41). 'Rights talk', as Harvey (2007, 178) has observed, was in an important sense the natural outcome of the resistance struggles generated by neo-liberal imperialism:

> Dispossession…is fragmented and particular – a privatization here, an environmental degradation there, a financial crisis of indebtedness somewhere else. It is hard to oppose all of this specificity and particularity without appeal to universal principles. Dispossession entails the loss of rights. Hence the turn to a universalistic rhetoric of human rights, and the like, as the basis for a unified oppositional politics.

In France, during the 1980s, prominent former leftists such as Bernard Henri-Levy, Andre Glucksman and Bernard Kouchner began to champion 'humanitarian intervention' as a solution to Third World hunger, medical emergencies and the suffering of civilian victims of war. An earlier flirtation with anti-imperialist politics had now given way to a deeply Eurocentric ethics of caring and compassion. Action needed to be taken, but the only ones with human agency were the Western saviours. The figure of the revolutionary anti-colonial militant was replaced by the helpless victim of famine and civil war. New imperial subjects were being reimagined, stripped of a history or politics of their own and utterly dependent on the good works of their First-World liberators:

> The new figuration of the victim occurs in a regime of pure actuality created by the rhetoric of emergency, an eternal present that not only dispossesses the victim of her own history, but removes her from history itself. In the new politics of emotion, subject and object are described in different, indeed invidious terms, with the objects of the relationship – the victims – having distinctive and distinctly less equal, qualities than the subjects of the West. In fact, to call it a politics of emotion is a misnomer. For, to what extent can the figure of suffering – the new generic figure of alterity in the 1980s and 1990s appearing nightly on television screens in the West – lead in and of itself to a politics. Are pity and moral indignation political emotions?
>
> Ross (2007, 163)

In an atmosphere in which the 'rhetoric of emergency' had trumped political analysis, it was a short step from 'quasi military acts of rescue and the emergency landing of doctors' to outright support for 'humanitarian' military intervention. That this was, in truth, a latter-day version of 'the white man's burden' was not the point; both Left and Right had found the necessary 'moral and spiritual supplement' (Ross 2007, 155) for both the prosecution of the 'war on terror' *and* for the rebranding of imperialism as an act of humanitarian benevolence.[5]

The doctrine of the 'responsibility to protect' (R2P) vulnerable populations by military means was first mooted by NGOs like *médecins san frontiers* (MSF), under the tutelage of Bernard Kouchner and others from the 1980s onward. Codified by the UN in 2005 with the support of the Bush administration, R2P represented a singular moment in which advocates of humanitarian intervention and defenders of 'preemptive' military action could celebrate their joint triumph. R2P doctrine has now become the vehicle through which NGOs and aid organizations have been integrated into military operations. In 2001, Colin Powell had referred to NGOS and aid workers as 'a force multiplier for us … an important part of our combat team' (quoted in Wiezman 2011, 52). By the time of the invasion of Iraq, the integration of aid agencies into the counter-insurgency strategies of the US military and its NATO allies was openly acknowledged (Foley 2008, 118). During the wars in Iraq and Afghanistan, counter-insurgency was seen as part of an all-encompassing and seamless effort involving military pacification, 'nation-building' and 'economic development'.[6] The new counter-insurgency strategy announced by the US military in 2005, by General David Petraeus, garnered an enthusiastic reception from Harvard University's Care Center for Human Rights (Weizman 2011, 17). Many NGOs inserted themselves directly into the counter-insurgency project; in 2011, the Canadian International Development Agency (CIDA) listed as its funding priorities, along with refugee assistance and clean water, the establishment of 'law and order by building the capacity of the Afghan National Army and Police and support (for) complementary efforts in areas of justice and corrections' (http://www.afghanistan.gc.ca). NGOs which are heavily reliant on state funding have been forced to accede to these priorities or have had their funding curtailed.[7] As Conor Foley (2008, 111) observes of his experience in Afghanistan: 'While some aid workers complained about the mixing of military and humanitarian mandates, the simple fact was that we were becoming objectively indistinguishable.'

Many aid workers, Michel Agier contends, have simply become 'a distant and delegated form of management, a government without citizens' (quoted in Weizman, 56–57). Refugee camps have become zones of exclusion and migration control in which refugee populations are warehoused far from Western shores:

> Displaced populations become the concern of the international community precisely because of the risks they potentially pose. The fear of migration, crime, and terrorism is conceived of as being in inverse relation to the well-being of populations. This tendency is best captured by the term 'human security' under which every dimension of human life – from food and shelter to education – is measured within a shifting calculus of risk.
>
> Weizman (2011, 57)

A common thread we have been tracing throughout has been how the 'risk management' language of finance capital, like the commodity form from which it derives, has come to shape nearly every aspect of life – from the market-determined subjects of neo-liberal citizenship to the prosecution of imperial warfare. As Weizman demonstrates, this same discourse has now woven itself into the fabric of International Humanitarian Law (IHL) through the codification of the principle of proportionality, i.e. that a balance should be struck between military objectives and damage to civilian lives and property. In practice, however, it has become a highly legalistic forensics of 'legitimate' suffering in which the calculus of who deserves to live and who deserves to die can be measured according to the same risk management algorithms which predict financial success or failure. In other words, not very well:

> Like the finance specialists who acknowledge the impossibility of prediction but do little else than calculate, the economists of violence are incessantly weighing their options and hedging their risks under the assumption of unpredictability and uncertainty. It is the very act of calculation – the very fact that calculation took place – that justifies their action. Indeterminacy, the very principle that makes the economics of liberal capitalism generate profit, or burst after a sequence of failures, is also central to the conduct and potential outcomes of the contemporary wars.
>
> Weizman (2011, 12)

Israel has been one of the pioneers of this new science of proportional suffering and Gaza has been its laboratory. Because IHL is based on the common law tradition of legal precedent, the ongoing occupation of Palestine has provided the Israelis with a unique role in the evolution of the IHL. As Asa Kasher (quoted in Weizman, 2011, 93), a professor of ethics at Tel Aviv University, boasted:

> The more often Western states apply principles that originated in Israel to their own non-traditional conflicts in places like Afghanistan and Iraq, then the greater the chance these principles have of becoming a valuable part of international law. What we *do* becomes the law.

The Israeli army has long applied the proportional principle of calorie rationing as a cheap means for controlling the population of Gaza. A military document, revealingly titled *Red Lines*, sets out in careful detail the 'humanitarian' minimum caloric intake for adult males, women and children in Gaza. The idea was to calculate the minimum number of international aid trucks allowed in to Gaza to sustain the bare survival of the population. A similar calculus of proportional suffering has been applied to the provision of medical equipment as well as the amount of diesel fuel allowed to power Gaza's only power plant. The 2008–2009 invasion of Gaza was unprecedented for the way in which humanitarian law was consciously mobilized and rewritten by the Israeli military. The use of white phosphorus on heavily populated areas or allowing the slaughter of civilians after 'warning' them to flee an impending attack – all detailed in the UN-sponsored Goldstone report – served a double purpose for the Israelis:

> The invasion … did two simultaneous and seemingly paradoxical things: it both violated the law and aimed to shift its thresholds. This kind of violence not only transgresses but also attacks the very idea of rigid limits. In this circular logic, the illegal turns legal through continuous violation. There is indeed a 'law making character' inherent in military violence. This is the law in action, legislative violence as seen from the perspective of those who write it in practice.
>
> Weizman (2011, 94)

This analysis confirms an uncomfortable truth about the relationship between the IHL and contemporary imperialism. Drawing on Pashukanis's analysis of the legal subject, China Miéville has forcefully argued that the same principles which underpin capitalist property law also apply to the international legal relations between states. Like the formal equality between autonomous legal subjects in civil society, relations between states *appear* to be founded on the principle of equality. However, as with the citizenship illusion, formal equality masks an underlying inequality of power and violence:

> The fundamental subjects of international law are sovereign states, which face each other as property owners, each with sole proprietary ownership of their own territory, just as legal subjects in domestic law face each other as owners of commodities …The means of violence remains in the hand of the very parties disagreeing over the interpretation of law. 'There is here, therefore, an antinomy, of right against right, both equally bearing the seal of the law of exchange. *Between equal rights, force decides.*' And of course that force, the capacity for coercive violence that underpins the legal relation, is not distributed equally … *The international legal form assumes juridical equality and unequal violence.*
>
> Miéville (2006, 292)

How is it that the discourse of human rights has become the accomplice of empire? And what does it tell us about the kind of citizen-subjects it envisions? One answer to this question lies in the very definition of liberal democracy itself. As Ellen Wood (Wood 2006, 19) has observed:

> The essence of democracy as conceived in the U.S.A. is the coupling of formal democracy with substantive class rule. This involves a delicate

conceptual balancing act between an assertion of popular sovereignty –
government of, by, and for the people – and the dominance of capital,
the subordination of politics to capitalist markets, and imperatives of
profit…As the founding fathers intended, we think of political rights as
essentially passive, and citizenship as a passive, individual, even private
identity, which may express itself by voting from time to time but which has
no active, collective or social meaning…So there is nothing immediately
implausible to most Americans about applying the idea of democracy to
imperialism.

During the Cold War, US imperialism was based on a model of capital
accumulation through the expansion of wage-labour. This was the substrate
upon which a form of 'national individualism' which closely aligned the values
of the individual with those of the imperial nation-state rested. National
individualism was rooted in notions of national solidarity, individual opportunity
and social rights. National security was equated with security of the American
empire and with the economic and social security of the individual (O'Connor
1984, 226). Thus it was that many of the oppositional organizations of the
working class – trade unions and social democratic parties – which gained
in strength and influence during this period saw no contradiction between
pressuring the state for expanded social rights *and* supporting imperialist
adventures in other countries.

Contemporary neo-liberal imperialism offers no such prospect. When the
social citizenship contract is being broken throughout the advanced capitalist
world, there can be no promise of actually *improving* the lives of those it sets
out to rescue, let alone of those who it persuades to fight its wars. Liberals
have aligned themselves with contemporary imperialism not because of its
domestic or international promise to expand social rights and equality but
for other reasons entirely. As Corey Robin has shown, the liberalism which
emerged from the 1960s was a confused amalgam of anxieties surrounding
the relationship between the liberal subject and various 'others' (groups,
nations) expressed in debates about identity and difference; social inclusion
and exclusion; and social cohesion and its opposite, social disintegration.
Conceiving of society in horizontal rather than vertical terms, they have tended
to think in terms of centres and margins; borders and threats. Because of the
ever-present danger of disintegration, of the self and the society, liberals have
tended to prefer integrative over conflictual forms of political sociability. Non-
political civil society organizations such as bowling clubs or boy scouts are
preferable to social activism and street demonstrations. But by the 1990s, it
was becoming apparent that the post-60s 'liberalism of anxiety' was a rather
thin soup on which to subsist:

Whatever their value as modes of social integration, these organizations are not weapons of social conflict or training grounds of strenuous selfhood. They may be partial to conversation and cocktails, perhaps some cooperative coping, but they eschew antagonism, conflict, and political confrontation. Civil society must thus remain a permanent disappointment for its defenders. Because it disappoints, its advocates are drawn to embrace an alternative ethos, the liberalism of terror... the liberalism of terror provides the bracing resolve and militant politics liberals of anxiety see but cannot find in private associations, civil society, and conversations about the weather.

Robin (2004, 142)

Well before 9/11, the atavistic threat of irrational terror had become a major trope in liberal and conservative thought. Ethnic genocide, for example, was explained in psychological and cultural terms as either a cultural revolt against a vaguely defined 'modernity' or an eruption of narcissistic fear of 'the other'. In the hands of writers such as Robert Kaplan, Samuel Huntington and Michael Iganatieff, terror was something that emerged from outside the sphere of politics and history and therefore provided the perfect pretext for political renewal for both liberals and conservatives (Robin 2004, 153). This spirit of renewal was nowhere more evident than in Samantha Power's book, *A Problem from Hell*, on the US response to the genocides in Rwanda and later the Bosnian conflict. In these instances, Power (quoted in Reiff 2005, 163) lamented 'that the forward looking, consoling refrain of "never again", a testament to America's can-do spirit, never grappled with the fact that the country had done nothing, practically or politically, to prepare itself to respond to genocide'. For Power, genocidal terror entailed a new moral imperative to act, with force if necessary, to save innocent lives. Employing a largely apolitical understanding of the roots of genocide, Power remained blind to the possibility that US power might be guilty of its own acts of genocide. Although critical of tactics of both Bush regimes, she was not prepared to label the Clinton administration's sanctions and bombing campaign against Iraq, which claimed hundreds of thousands of lives, an act of genocide. This was not an oversight on Power's part but a systematic blindness to US complicity in genocide, from Guatemala to East Timor (Seymour 2012, 219). For Power and other liberals, the Bosnian wars were the crucible upon which their conversion to 'humanitarian' military intervention was forged:

What the new wars of ethnic purity – and the corresponding duty of imperial involvement – promised for the Left as well as the Right was nothing less than the regeneration of the West. For liberals terror offered a posture of militant, crusading purpose, an opportunity to impose the Enlightenment abroad precisely because it could not be defended at home. For conservatives, it was a chance to restore martial valor and aristocratic heroism jeopardized by the free market and end of the Cold War. Whatever the source of their new fervor, Left and Right were now united in a worldwide revolutionary project to bring America to the rest of the world. This was not the first time that western intellectuals had looked to terror abroad for answers to their own domestic despair. It would not be the last.

Robin (2004, 155)

After 9/11, 'humanitarian' imperialism came fully into its own; the 'war on terror' was justified by liberals as a 'lesser evil' in the face of Islamist threats to Western values. In his book *The Lesser Evil*, Ignatieff (2004) attempted to give philosophical weight to the argument by acknowledging that the use of torture, violence and the suspension of civil liberties are 'evil' but still justified in certain circumstances. As Weizman (2011, 9) observes, 'it is through this use of the lesser evil that societies that see themselves as democratic can maintain regimes of occupation and neo-colonization'. Lesser evilism has now become the default position to justify everything from drone strikes, domestic spying, targeted assassinations, torture and proxy wars to full-scale military intervention. Yet, 'the logic is childishly simple to comprehend. Every evil that one endorses is the "lesser evil"' (Seymour 2012, 250). That the sum of such actions may cumulatively add up to a greater evil since they are committed and sanctioned by the world's most powerful states, is something few adherents of lesser evilism have been willing to acknowledge (Weizman 2011, 10). Early advocates of military intervention in the Balkans, like David Rieff (2005, 169), have concluded that the entire vocabulary of human rights has been compromised: 'The real lesson is that human rights – the secular religion of the West as Michael Ignatieff and others rightly called it – cannot provide any serious opposition to the American empire because human rights has become, however inconsistently applied, the official ideology of the American empire ....' Others have tried to sustain a concept of lesser evilism shorn of its imperial overtones. But in order to do this, they have had to adopt a language of 'bare life' in which the only permissible type of intervention is ministering to the broken bodies of those most afflicted by the ravages of war and neo-liberalism. Rony Brauman (quoted in Weizman 2011, 55), former president of MSF, has defended a minimalist humanitarianism that 'takes no political stand, makes no claim to transform society, and doesn't come to make war or peace, promote economic development, help administer justice, or export democracy or human rights values'. However laudable such minimalism may be as a critique of 'humanitarian' imperialism, it has less to offer as a political alternative. For that, we will need to look elsewhere.

Notes

1   www.reuters.com, 'U.S. will put more warships in Asia: Panetta', sourced 8/20/12.

2   Adam Hanieh (2010, 70) persuasively argues:

> As a constituting force in the hierarchies of the world-economy, the Gulf circuits of capital are tightly integrated with value-flows at the global level. They have thereby become central to the stability of global capitalism – underpinning the dominance of US-capitalism within the overall system – and will be essential to the reconfiguration of capitalist power in the wake of the financial crisis... It will be key to the form that imperialism's domination of the Middle-East region takes in the future – including of any potential challenger to US-power.

3   This figure is roughly in line with estimates by independent monitors such as the British Bureau of Investigative Journalism, the New America Foundation and the Long War Journal (Siddiqui 2013).

4   On the latter, long-time champions of the 'right of interference' like the French intellectual, Bernard Henri-Levi (Seymour 2012, 294) jubilantly declared, 'For the first time this concept was endorsed by the Arab League, by the African Union and by the UN security council. This is huge.'

5   Eyal Weizman (2011, 37–38) similarly traces the origins of French 'humanitarian' imperialism to the influence of Maoism in the 1960s. Freighted with a heavy dose of moralism, Maoism imbued many of its cadres with voluntaristic politics of the emergency:

> Many of these young activists and writers replaced an abstract concept of political 'justice' with an emotive idea of 'compassion', a revolutionary politics with one whose finite and practical goals are the relief of suffering in those regions of the world where it is most visible. The culture of immediate and direct action was easily transferred to the humanitarian culture of emergency.

6   As the US Army's Counterinsurgency Manual published in 2006 states: 'counterinsurgents aim to enable a country or regime to provide the security and rule of law that allow establishment of social services and growth of economic activity. COIN (counterinsurgency) thus involves the application of national power in the political, military, economic, social, information, and infrastructure fields and disciplines' (Headquarters of the Department of the Army, December 2006).

7   The Canadian government terminated funding to the faith-based human rights organization Kairos, through its international development agency, CIDA, as later admitted by a government minister, for its support of Palestinian human rights (*Globe and Mail*, 3rd December 2009).

4

States of Security: From Social Security to the Security State

US nationalism and liberal imperialism have always gone hand in hand. This coupling is key to understanding the link between the 'national security' goals of the imperialist state and the formation of individual and collective political identities associated with citizenship. Presented to the world in the form of a benign universalism, the coupling of national identity with the global aspirations of US capitalism has always been premised on a considerable dose of ideological and physical coercion. Such aspirations were often brutally crushed in the name of an overarching and much more powerful national project which closely linked 'national security' to national and patriotic identities which fit with the underlying interests of American capitalism.

During the New Deal era, 'social security' in the form of expanded state provision of social welfare was linked to other national security goals, most notably securing the necessary markets and conditions for the expanded reproduction of capital. State intervention in the domestic sphere altered working-class expectations and considerably undermined more radical proposals for social transformation. Workers could now enjoy enhanced citizenship rights in the form of labour rights and social provision but only as a means linking them more firmly to the expanding fortunes of private capital.

A good illustration of this was the way in which Roosevelt's Federal Housing Administration (FHA) not only laid the groundwork for the expansion of the largely white middle-class suburbs, leaving African Americans to languish in inner city slums for decades to come, but also underwrote the vast expansion of the private mortgage industry.

At the same time, it inured American workers to the still unfamiliar world of long-term debt:

> Through the attempts to stabilize a faltering economy, New Deal housing programs radically changed existing consumer and business practices of debt. Borrowers enthusiastically took longer mortgages as large institutional lenders enjoyed insured investments. These radical interventions in mortgage markets fundamentally altered the ways in which Americans borrowed… Moreover, this debt was not of the personal kind to which they had been accustomed, but to large impersonal corporations. Debtors gradually became accustomed to owing money in large amounts to someone they had never met.
>
> Hyman (2011, 72)

This phase of the debt economy not only linked the idea of economic security to the security of capital but also helped foster the kind of subjective dispositions conducive to hard work, paying one's debts and saving for the future. Past labours would be rewarded by future security provided one stuck to the script being written by the state and corporate capital. The new ethos of social citizenship was thus 'a liberal police power *par excellence* in being used to secure the existing state of corporate capital and fashion around it appropriate behaviour patterns on the part of its subjects and agents. As well as securing the state, "social security" easily became a mechanism for simultaneously securing capital' (Neocleous 2008, 90).

Social security was thus conceived from the beginning as part and parcel of a larger architecture of national security and empire. It was designed to foster the attitudes, beliefs and patterns of social behaviour which accorded with the evolving parameters of liberal citizenship. In general, political activity was to be restricted to the largely passive realm of liberal citizenship, while industrial struggle was channelled into the contractual technicalities of wages and working conditions. Greater state involvement in social life was designed to pacify more radical claims on the economy by containing them within the political sphere. New civic and social rights could be expanded to formerly excluded groups without threatening the private powers of capital. Thus, the emerging social security state represented a powerful moral technology of governance and citizenship within the larger context of post-Second World War capitalism:

> In *practical* terms 'security' legitimized some limited working-class demands *vis-a-vis* the capitalist economy and could thereby satisfy the demands of large numbers of radicals and socialists. At the same time, however, it also satisfied middle-class desires and was turned to the

advantage of corporations legitimating the latter's place in the modern polity. In *theoretical* terms, 'security' had become central to the dominant ideology, if not *the* dominant idea itself; the modern capitalist social formation had gone some way to becoming 'securitized'.

Neocleous (2008, 90–91)

But if the velvet glove of social security represented one side of the equation, it also masked a darker, more coercive side of the national security state – one which reinforced a paranoid style of politics which remains a hallmark of American political culture to this day. This was evident in a host of forms, from restrictive trade union laws and strike-breaking; a prison-industrial complex which continues to disproportionately imprison blacks, Native Americans and Latinos; to the hounding and blacklisting of communists, gays and lesbians. With the beginning of the Cold War, suspect individuals and organizations were placed on a Security Index which by 1954 totalled over 26,000 names (Neocleous 2008, 110). Those who were considered 'un-American' were subjected to a range of sanctions, from loss of employment to social ostracism to imprisonment. The Campaign for Truth (launched in early 1950, quickly followed by the NSC 68) set out in no uncertain terms the ideological and material terrain on which the Cold War would be fought:

Every institution of our society is an instrument which it (Communism) is sought to stultify and turn against our purposes. Those that touch most closely our material and moral strength are obviously all the prime targets, labor unions, civic enterprises, schools, churches, and all media influencing opinion. The effort is not so much to make them serve obvious Soviet ends as to prevent them from serving our ends, and thus to make them sources of confusion in our economy, our culture and our body politic.

quoted in Neocleous (2008, 109)

The House Committee on Un-American Activities (HUAC) hearings presided over by Senator Joseph McCarthy in the late 1940s and the early 1950s (but with a much longer history reaching back to 1934 and forward to 1975) represented the most public and spectacular example of the campaign to define loyalty and national identity in terms of national security goals. It was an ideology which defined what it was to be American in the lurid language of what was 'un-American', namely any world view which questioned the verities of private property, the state and capitalist morality. The combined weight of the Hoey Committee Report of 1950 titled *Employment of Homosexuals and Other Sex Perverts in Government* and the Truman Administrations Loyalty Program promulgated in 1953 was to ferret out those with leftist sympathies and gays from government employment. Thus it was that government loyalty boards quizzed employees on whether they believed that the Red Cross should desegregate its blood supply and whether federal anti-lynching legislation was required – both of which were policies advocated by the American Communist Party. Affirmative answers were grounds for investigation or firing (Robin 2004, 184).

Scholars, intellectuals and artists were generously funded through a variety of methods to preach the new gospel of anti-communism. Federal Bureau of Investigation director J. Edgar Hoover deemed it essential to co-opt 'people who think' into the anti-communist crusade and personally wrote sixty articles in legal reviews and other professional publications supporting this view (Robin 2004, 186). At the international level, George Kennan, the architect of the post-Second World War Marshall Plan, had introduced the concept of the 'necessary lie' and directed the CIA to undertake covert psychological operations in support of American anti-communist activities. By 1949, disaffected former Trotskyists such as Sidney Hook, James Burnham and Dwight MacDonald were organizing against Soviet influence in the cultural field with funding from the CIA. In Britain, the Information Research Department (IRD) followed a similar strategy by distributing fact sheets with the help of former Communists such as Arthur Koestler, who had become disaffected with the Soviet Union following the Hitler–Stalin Pact in 1939. In Berlin in 1949, Koestler and Melvin J. Lasky, a prominent German intellectual who had collaborated closely with the Western occupation forces, organized the Berlin Congress on Cultural Freedom in June 1950 with funding from the US Office of Policy Coordination. The Congress was enough of a success to be added to the CIA's 'Propaganda Assets Inventory'. The bulk of the CIA money in Europe – about $200 million per year – came from the Marshall Plan funding formula which allocated 50 per cent of the fifty-fifty funding split between the US and the recipient nations to a 'counter-part fund' (Saunders 1999).

According to the CIA operative Michael Josselson, the 'greatest asset' in the cultural Cold War was the magazine *Encounter* which ran from 1953 to 1990. Initially co-edited by the British poet Stephen Spender and the American Irving Kristol, *Encounter* set the tone for the executions of Julius and Ethel Rosenberg by arguing that they were guilty as charged and that the American legal system was fair and just. Through the Congress of Cultural Freedom, Josselson pursued an agenda which saw the birth of similar publications in Australia, India, Japan, China, Africa and the Arab world and sold itself as a 'serious alliance of intellectuals committed to demonstrating the fallibility of the Soviet mythos, and the superiority of Western democracy as a framework for cultural and philosophical inquiry' (quoted in Saunders 1999, 213).

The 'necessary lie' that the CIA was bankrolling both *Encounter* and the Congress of Cultural Freedom took its toll on those whose job it was to sustain the subterfuge. Many authors, and some of its editors, notably Stephen Spender and Frank Kermode, were unaware of the CIA funding. In 1967, *Ramparts* magazine, despite a strenuous CIA-led smear campaign, finally revealed the truth, prompting Josselson to resign from both the magazine and the Congress. Several other architects of the clandestine state committed suicide. By 1975, with the revelations of the Church Committee Hearings, the full scope of US covert operations came fully into public view.[1] The Church Committee revealed the CIA's long history of targeted assassinations of foreign political figures deemed hostile to US interests, including Patrice Lumumba of the Democratic Republic of Congo, the Diem brothers of Vietnam, Rene Schneider of Chile and Rafael Trujillo of the Dominican Republic. It also documented CIA participation in the 1973 overthrow of the Allende regime in Chile. Domestically, the Committee drew back the curtain on COINTELPRO (Counter Intelligence Program) which covertly targeted a range of political, civil rights and anti-war activists. Techniques deployed included infiltration of 'subversive' political groups, the use of psychological operations and smear campaigns, legal harassment and targeted assassinations. Not only were more moderate Civil Rights leaders like Martin Luther King systematically targeted through electronic bugging, others like Black Panther Party leader Fred Hampton were murdered in an orchestrated shoot-out with Chicago police. As the Church Committee concluded:

Many of the techniques used would be intolerable in a democratic society even if all of the targets had been involved in violent activity, but COINTELPRO went far beyond that...the Bureau conducted a sophisticated vigilante operation aimed squarely at preventing the exercise of First Amendment rights of speech and association, on the theory that preventing the growth of dangerous groups and the propagation of dangerous ideas would protect the national security and deter violence.

Soon enough, there would be renewed longing for the ideological certainties which fuelled the permissive practices of the Cold War security regime. But, as Stoner Saunders (1999, 427) reminds us:

Behind the 'unexamined nostalgia for the "Golden Days" of American intelligence' lay a much more devastating truth: the same people who read Dante and went to Yale and were educated in civic virtue recruited Nazis, manipulated the outcome of democratic elections, gave LSD to unwitting subjects, opened the mail of thousands of American citizens, overthrew governments, supported dictatorships, plotted assassinations, and engineered the Bay of Pigs disaster. 'In the name of what?' asked one critic. 'Not civic virtue, but Empire.'

The first phase of the US security state left at least some liberal members of the political establishment worried about the dangers of surveillance and the atmosphere of distrust it generated, especially when it came to its own citizens. Senator Church mused about the dangers of a future tyranny in which the technological capacity of the security services would allow 'it to impose total tyranny, and there would be no way to fight back because the most careful effort to combine together in resistance to the government, no matter how privately it was done, is within the reach of the government to know. Such is the capability of this technology' (Senator Frank Church speech). But, the prospect of such a scenario would not require a tyrannical regime in the literal sense; the reality, when it did arrive, would prove much more prosaic and find all of the justification it required in a nominally democratic political system which still prided itself on 'the rule of law'. The interregnum represented by the Church Committee hearings and the Executive Orders (11905 and 12036) issued by the Ford and Carter administrations respectively, limiting covert operations, was short lived. The Reagan administration would soon reverse whatever progress had been made to reign in the growing powers of the security state. Henceforth, the original link between social security and national security would be irretrievably severed. With the shift to neo-liberalism under Reagan, social acquiescence in the broad goals of national security would come to rely less on the promise of the good life for its citizens and much more directly on the politics of fear.

National security, rational choice and social capital

An important coda to this history is the political role played by a consortium of security-intellectuals whose influence clearly demonstrates the elective affinity which existed between the build-up of the US security apparatus and early formulations of neo-liberal ideology. In 1950, the Rand Corporation brought together a group of defence analysts under the tutelage of mathematician Albert Wohlstetter, often considered the father of neoconservatism. Among them was the economist Kenneth Arrow, formulator of rational choice theory, which was seen – in Cold War terms – as an alternative world view to Soviet communism. Arrow asserted that any attempt by any decision-making body with at least two players and faced with at least three possible outcomes could not result in consensus. Arrow believed that he had successfully uncovered the fallacy at the heart of all forms of collectivist ideologies by demonstrating that all social processes are reducible to individual preferences:

> At its most basic, Arrow's work demonstrated in formal terms – that is, in mathematical expression – that collective rational group decisions are logically impossible. Arrow's paradox, or Arrow's impossibility theorem, as it came to be called, presented an unshakeable mathematical argument that destroyed the academic validity of most kinds of social compact. Arrow utilized his findings to concoct a value system based on economics that destroyed the Marxist notion of collective will … Arrow assumed that individuals were rational, that they had consistent preferences that they sought to maximize for their own selfish benefit. Arrow also assumed that reason as he defined it, was not culturally relative but identical in all human beings, who act according to the same rules of logic … Simply put, he posited that immutable, incontrovertible science tells us the collective is nothing, the individual is all.
>
> Abella (2009, 51)

Arrow's formulations cast the arms race between the superpowers as a zero-sum game in which agreement was unlikely and therefore the best course of action for any state was to pursue its rational self-interest. This idea would soon spread to everything from public policy to corporate behaviour and become the dominant ideology in mainstream economics and political science for several decades. The proponents of rational choice theory would play a role in several presidential administrations from Eisenhower to George W. Bush. The Randites would conduct studies which justified the Reagan government's privatization schemes, deregulation, lower taxes and attacks on trade union rights. Nobel Prizes were conferred on several alumni, including Gary Becker and Paul Samuelson (Abella 2008, 258–259). Becker was one of the chief intellectual colonizers of academic disciplines beyond economics, including sociology, criminology, anthropology and demography. According to Becker's reductionist logic, neoclassical economics provided the template for understanding all human societies at any point in human history: 'From a methodological viewpoint, the aim … is to show how what is considered important in the sociological and anthropological literature can be usefully analyzed when incorporated into the framework provided by economic theory' (Becker quoted in Fine 2001, 44). Becker sought the main motivations for human behaviour within the asocial realm of individual preferences rooted in rational behaviours which he believed derived from human evolution. There was very little room in this model for external norms and values of a social nature. James Coleman, Becker's colleague at the University of Chicago, sought to deal with the issue of 'the social' by scaling upward from individual preferences to the 'macro level' via the concept of 'aggregation', a concept derived from economics. Coleman coined the term 'social capital' to capture the way market imperfections and public goods and bads can be accounted for through a rational choice framework:

> It merely represents the extent to which an appropriate solution has been found to the problem of public goods (from which all can consume without cost but none has an incentive to provide unless charging an efficiently high cost) and externalities (where the actions of individuals have direct repercussions for others). The capacity to deal with these issues reflects a balance between satisfying individual interests and exercising control over them (to prevent free-riding). Once such arrangements are internalized by individuals, they represent norms of behaviour.
>
> Fine (2001, 74)

Despite its ostensible social starting point, Coleman's framework remains rooted in rational choice, with a strong emphasis on the ways in which individual behaviours can be controlled through market-like incentives and rewards. In short, the concept of social capital professes to have found the missing link uniting individual and social behaviours by demonstrating how an 'as if market' operates in non-market situations (Fine 2001, 79).

Via the concept of social capital, rational choice theory was to have an appeal far beyond the ranks of neoclassical economics. By the 1990s, its proponents would be welcomed into the White House and taken up in the World Bank and the theory would entrench itself as the *theory du jour* throughout the social sciences. Social capital would come to be seen as the panacea for global poverty and gender inequality and as the precondition for democracy and economic development worldwide. It would also dovetail neatly with conservative accounts which sought to explain economic backwardness and success in terms of culture, religion and politics. For many liberals, it would become the basis for a new conception of citizenship anchored in the self-help ethos of voluntary associations and social exchange. In political terms, it would become the academic equivalent of so-called Third Way social democracy, which sought to portray the middle ground between the state and the market as a newfound realm of freedom (Fine 2001, 95). As such, social capital provided the optimistic face of neo-liberal financialization. Moreover, as a theoretical rationale for those NGOs which had allied themselves with the forces of empire, it would lend a further patina of legitimacy to 'humanitarian' imperialism. Despite repeated and devastating critique, it has continued its zombie-like march within academic and non-academic circles alike, suggesting that more powerful ideological forces are at work.

In his widely influential work, Robert Putnam (1994) deployed the concept of social capital to assert the importance of civic associations, trust, norms and networks, in explaining the differences between the undeveloped south of Italy and its industrialized northern regions. In his bestselling book, *Bowling Alone: The Collapse and Revival of American Community* (2001), he sought to apply the same analysis to the decline of civic life in the US since the 1950s. Strong stocks of social capital, according to Putnam, are seen as a sign of a healthy polity and the lack of such stocks a symptom of unhealthiness and instability. By focusing on such horizontal relations as associational activity and civic engagement, Putnam managed to ignore the role of vertical factors such as neo-liberal restructuring and the decline of the welfare state (Edwards and Foley in Fine 2001, 93). Questions of class and state power, gender and racial oppression, internal colonialism, social control and conflict do not figure in the theory of social capital: 'social capital without the capitalist system in other words' (Fine 2001, 95). As Sydney Tarrow observed in his critique of Putnam, by reducing social capital to the micro-level of socio-psychological factors such as associational activity and trust and by ignoring macro-level vertical structures of power, Putnam mistakes the symptoms of social malaise for the cause (Tarrow 1996). The methodological individualism inherited from rational choice theory thus results in an analysis which is ahistorical, asocial and mechanistic.

This is most obvious in the way in which civil society is conceived by social capital theory. Associations and civic institutions are seen as agents of 'social cohesion' and unfettered social exchange. Not only does this benign view ignore the darker side of associational activity – what are we to make of neo-fascist organizations? – it also drastically underestimates the extent to which civil society is the terrain upon which class and other forms of social power are fought out. As Antonio Gramsci argued, civil society is a vast 'trench work' of institutions and organizations, many of which are dedicated to maintaining class domination and control. Lacking any coherent economic theory of its own, save that which it has borrowed from neoclassical economics, social capital theorists associate coercion almost entirely with the state. They forget that state coercion in capitalist societies tends to favour the interests of private capital and that the market involves its own distinctive forms of coercion. The market needs to be understood 'not simply as a sphere of opportunity, freedom and choice, but as a compulsion, a necessity, a social discipline, capable of subjecting all human activities and relationships to its requirements' (Wood 1995, 252).

The origins of social capital theory in the rational choice doctrines of the post-Second World War security state no doubt have long been forgotten by its present-day practitioners. However, blindness to the mutually reinforcing forms of state and market power in contemporary capitalism means that its usefulness for a theory of citizenship is extremely limited. At its worst, it has become an elaborate theoretical apologia for neo-liberalism and the politics of empire. Finally, social capital's ongoing commitment to methodological individualism means that it is ill-equipped to make sense of the very thing it seeks to explain: the collective behaviours and solidarities which move ordinary people. But for the originators of rational choice, this was a deliberate move:

> Their choice of instrument has unleashed world-changing responses driven precisely by the forces their instrument cannot handle – religions, nationalism, patriotism. Moreover, deliberately or not, rational choice theory has become a handy rhetorical weapon for groups whose political and financial aims are to reconstruct the social system of the United States – returning it to its pre-New Deal days, while making billions in the process.
>
> Abella (2009, 309)

By making invisible the very processes it sought to justify – the supremacy of private capital backed by an all-powerful security and military apparatus – rational choice theory would perform one of the central tasks of ideology, which is to mystify and naturalize the sources of social power. In doing so it has helped to foster a culture of political fear which continues to pursue its 'terror' demons in all of the wrong places.

A political economy of fear

One of the chief benefits of the separation of the economic and political spheres in liberal capitalist societies is that it provides the state with the appearance of neutrality, of standing above the fray of competing interests in civil society. State violence, rather than representing particular class interests, seems to be deployed in the name of the public good. The state takes on a fetish-like character disguising the mutually reinforcing division of labour between the coercive powers of the state and those of capital. Because it can claim to work through the impartial rule of law, when combined with the work of willing collaborators in civil society and the insecurities generated by the rule of capital, the liberal state is a particularly effective vehicle for the mobilization of political fear (Robin 2004, 199). As with international humanitarian law, what is done in the name of security is not some lawless aberration but something entirely consistent with legal norms and precedent. There simply is no distinction between 'exceptional' and 'normal' uses of the law. Liberal constitutions are sophisticated instruments of class rule designed to obscure and mystify their origins. To demand a return to the liberal 'rule of law' is to assume that law and force are distinct: 'emergency powers are deployed *for* the exercise of violence necessary for the permanent refashioning of order – the violence *of* law, not violence contra law' (Neocleous 2008, 73).

As we saw in the previous chapter, even before, but certainly after, the events of 9/11, many American liberals had been drawn towards a 'liberalism of terror' as a way of re-galvanizing the American polity in the wake of the collapse of communism. For them, terror had the advantage of clearing away the messy debris of political debate; it provided the sobering clarity of a call to arms, something which all political sides could agree upon. Political fear, in other words, was legitimate; the outside world really was a dangerous and scary place. Fear of 'the Other' has now become a permanent feature of American social life, whether the 'Other' was specified as the 'communist menace' or today as 'Islamic Terrorists' or immigrants. It has been consciously mobilized by powerful groups in the name of a 'security-identity-loyalty complex, held together by fear and violence' (Neocleous 2008, 141). From the National Security Act of 1947 to the Patriot Act of 2001, the discourse of 'national security' has played a key role in the articulation of American national identity and patriotism:

> the ideology of (national) security served and continues to serve as a means of delineating, framing and asserting identity. Security functions as a means not just for identifying and dealing with potential military threats, but also as a mechanism for the political constitution and cultural production of identity and, as such, for the unity of the political community.
>
> Neocleous (2008, 122)

Fear, therefore, plays an active role in the making of political subjectivities. It functions as a kind of middle term between consent and coercion; its peculiar power rests in the fact that it draws equally from both. Political fear seems to work best when those subjected to it have some belief in its validity. In both Stalin's show trials of the 1930s and the McCarthy witch-hunt in the US, many of those who were persecuted believed in the rightness of the charges against them even as they knew them to be false. In both instances, there was a heartfelt belief in the legitimacy of the very system which was the source of their fear. In this sense, as Corey Robin (2004, 174) argues, political fear is both rational and moral in that it combines a reasoned assessment of the consequences of acting against the institutions which are the source of fear with a moral commitment to those same institutions:

> Fear poses complex moral dilemmas … in which self-interest and moral principle cannot be easily separated. It is in this space that our teachers and preachers of fear work, throwing their weight behind one interest over another, making one principle seem higher than another.

How else to explain the kind of self-censorship which was commonly practiced in the mainstream media in the days and weeks following the events of 9/11 or in the run-up to the invasion of Iraq? *Wikileaks* revealed that *The Washington Post* held without releasing for nine months a copy of the 2007 video showing a US helicopter gunship shooting unarmed Iraqi civilians in Baghdad. They also reveal that the CBS programme *60 Minutes* had evidence of the torture of prisoners at Abu Ghraib by US soldiers for a year before making them public and only then because the journalist Seymour Hersh informed CBS that he would be publishing a piece on the affair in *The New Yorker* magazine. Of the media's role in the aftermath of 9/11, former CNN Executive Vice-President and General Manager Rena Golden commented:

> Anyone who claims the U.S. media didn't censor itself is kidding you. It wasn't a matter of government pressure but a reluctance to criticize anything in a war that was obviously supported by the vast majority of the people. And this isn't just a CNN issue – every journalist who was in any way involved in 9/11 is partly responsible.
>
> Gallagher (2013)

The former CBS anchor, Dan Rather explained his complicity and that of the media in general in the following terms:

> But when a tough question is asked and not answered, when reputable people come before the public and say, 'wait a minute, something's not right here', the press has treated them like voices crying in the wilderness. These views, though they might be given air time, become lone dots – dots that journalists don't dare connect, even if the connections are obvious, even if people on the internet and the independent press are making these

very same connections. The mainstream press doesn't connect these dots because someone might then accuse them of editorializing, or of being the, quote, 'liberal media'.

Mitchell (2013)

Small wonder that the former press secretary for George W. Bush, Scott McClellan, described the media as 'complicit enablers' in the months before the invasion of Iraq (Anees 2008). No doubt, as 'complicit enablers', Golden and Rather are indulging in some retrospective apologetics for their own actions while conveniently ignoring the power of the media to shape public opinion. But their rationalizations are telling because they both name a fear of the consequences of stepping outside the boundaries of mainstream public opinion or being labelled 'too liberal'. Fear of a right-wing backlash is real in both instances but so is an implicit belief in the legitimacy of such a reaction: 'fear and capitulation seem the rational and moral response to pressure' (Robin 2004, 169).

The disclosures by *Wikileaks,* Bradley (now Chelsea) Manning and Edward Snowden reveal the depth and breadth of the surveillance capabilities of the US security state. Under the provisions of the Patriot Act, the National Security Agency (NSA) has been able to collect an astonishing amount of information on friends and foes alike; not only do security agencies spy on enemy states but on allied heads of states as well. While Muslims and Arabs have received special attention, the US security state seems just as disposed to eavesdrop on the general population as it does on Al Qaeda operatives. The NSA's Prism programme, which employs powerful internet and cell phone tracking tools such as 'Boundless Informant' and 'Mainway', is able to collect billions of domestic and foreign cellphone, email and social media transactions daily, all with the apparent complicity of the corporations which provide such services. One cell carrier, Verizon, had set up a dedicated fibre-optic line from its main operation facility to a US military base in Quantico, Virginia, while AT&T reportedly kept a secret, high-security room reserved for the NSA (Risen and Lichtblau 2013). Between 2007 and 2012, Microsoft, Yahoo, Google, Facebook, YouTube, Skype, AOL and Apple, all joined the NSA programme (Greenwald and MacAskill 2013). Further, the Snowden files reveal that the NSA's 2013 budget requested funds for the creation of a repository which could collect twenty billion 'record events' daily and make them available to security analysts within one hour (Risen and Poitras 2013).

Although such revelations have sparked outrage, it is difficult to see how such knowledge can, on its own, contribute to the mobilization of sustained opposition. More likely is that such revelations will fuel even higher levels of political fear and anxiety. Political fear is fundamentally conservative in that it tends to reinforce existing inequalities of power and wealth. Ultimately, it is about maintaining systems of oppression and exploitation which rely upon the intersecting hierarchies of class, race and gender and has been mobilized historically when internal or external threats to the existing order appear imminent (Robin 2004, 179). In this light, the corporations which acceded to NSA requests for access to private data should be seen as willing collaborators in a common project rather than as reluctant bystanders. In this, the state and private capital have found common cause, each complicit in upholding a political economy of fear in which 'the ideology of (in)security is central to the political logic of capital as well as the logic of the state' (Neocleous 2008, 144). It is from the intersection of these twin logics that the politics of fear bleeds outward to permeate the rest of society.

The workplace remains a bastion of coercion and surveillance with few of the legal protections such as freedoms of speech, privacy and due process which apply to other areas of civil society. The workplace is where most citizens 'consistently encounter personal coercion and repressive fear' (Robin 2004, 228). The rise of contingent and precarious forms of work has only heightened these vulnerabilities. According to the US Bureau of Labor Statistics, about one in five employees are charged with supervisory functions (Smith 2013). Others have put the number at nearly double that amount (Robin 2004, 232). Nearly 75 per cent of US companies monitor their workers and it is estimated that twenty-seven million employees are monitored worldwide. Surveillance and monitoring range across performance, behaviour and personal attributes and include computer and telephone monitoring, mystery shoppers, location tracking, lie detectors, drug, biometric and genetic testing and data mining of personal information (Ball 2010). Using the new technologies available to them, employers have not been content simply to regulate their employees; they seem also to want to reach inside workers' minds and bodies to assert an even greater degree of control. The threat of terrorism has been used to further erode workplace protections. The Department of Homeland Security removed 'whistleblower' protection for its 170,000 employees as well as the right to form a union. Others followed suit, invoking the ethos of lean production as the reason for removing union and other protections from workers in the Department of Justice and the Transportation Security Administration. As Admiral James Loy argued:

> Fighting terrorism demands a flexible workforce that can rapidly respond to threats. That can mean changes in work assignments and other conditions of employment that are not compatible with the duty to bargain with unions.
>
> quoted in Robin (2004, 191)

The growing insecurity of life and work since the onset of the crisis in 2008 has provided fertile new ground for the politics of fear. The 'normalization of uncertainty' (Martin 2002, 145) has allowed fears and anxieties of all kinds to proliferate. Living with risk now embraces not just the fears associated with unemployment or mortgage default but the whole panoply of perceived threats associated with street crime, drugs, homelessness and domestic terror. Alongside the security state, and often working in close cooperation with it, the private security industry has also mushroomed.

The role of private military contractors in Iraq is well known. Private military suppliers such as Haliburton, Bechtel and over sixty other companies employing over 20,000 personnel supplied the US military with everything from missiles to meals. As one commentator noted,

> the private military industry has contributed more forces to Iraq than any other member of the U.S.-led coalition, being nearly equal to all the states excluding the U.S. combined. To be more accurate then, President Bush's claim of a 'Coalition of the Willing' might be renamed the 'Coalition of the Billing'.
>
> Singer (2005)

Most private contractors operated on 'cost-plus' contracts which meant that profits above costs were guaranteed. In 2004, the Haliburton subsidiary Kellogg, Brown and Root (KBR) overcharged the US military $61 million for fuel and another $27.4 million for food. Much of the labour that served in KBR kitchens was imported from South Asia and was paid a derisory $3.00 per day. Before having its contracts terminated by the Pentagon, Haliburton had $18.5 billion in contracts for the US military in Iraq (Doran 2012, 155–156).

Incarcerating large sections of the population, often in privately run prisons and immigration detention centres, has also become a big business. Since 1980, the US prison population has grown by 780 per cent. One in three African American men will spend time in prison at some point in their life (Filipovic 2013). One of the largest private prison corporations, Corrections Corporation of America (CCA), manages sixty-five prison and detention centres for the US government. Many of the contracts signed with CCA include 'occupancy requirements' which require state governments to maintain prisoner populations at between 80 and 100 per cent capacity, whether or not crime rates are falling (Kirby et al. 2013). Moreover, prisoners are compelled to work during their 'occupancy' by making uniforms for McDonald's and lingerie for Victoria's Secret, furniture and computer parts; and they are increasingly used in telemarketing and for drug testing. Without the encumbrance of unions, the right to strike or the usual workplace protections, prison labour has become the ultimate form of coerced labour under neo-liberalism (Neocleous 2008, 151–152). As McNally observes:

> It is instructive in this regard that, for all of their talk of 'freedom', neoliberals' preferred disciplinary institution has been the prison: it is there that the 'undisciplined', particularly young people of colour, are to be taught the price of not functioning as obedient cogs in the machinery of capitalist production … It is prisons and not schools or even job training programs – that secure the disciplinary ethos of neoliberalism.
>
> McNally (2011, 118–119)

The security fetish

Several authors (Neocleous 2008; Rigakos 2002; Spitzer 1987) have explored the relationship between processes of commodification and the private security industry. Spitzer reminds us that security commodities are different than most in that their use-value rests on a combination of risk calculation and faith in preventing what *may* happen. Preventing 'what may happen' is indeterminate since we can never know for sure that the security commodities purchased are responsible or not for preventing an unseen and unpredictable threat. But it is precisely the indeterminacy of such threats that freights security commodities with a strongly subjective and ideological element. Security is a conservative force with strong affinities to the negative liberties of classical liberal thought; it is not about challenging the existing order but rather 'freedom *from*' some unwelcome intrusion, usurpation, or limitation (Spitzer 1987, 48). Embedded as they are in a system in which all human needs and desires are mediated by the market, security commodities offer up a vast array of highly tailored, individual solutions for consumers with the ability to purchase them.

Through the gradual obliteration of non-market forms of security, capitalism turns insecurity into a permanent condition (Spitzer 1987, 47). Not only does the kind of freedom which arises from market dependence create ongoing insecurity for the worker – the freedom of 'working or starving' – but capitalism itself is characterized by 'constant revolutionizing of production, uninterrupted disturbance of all social relations, everlasting certainty and agitation' (Marx and Engels 1972, 63). The security industry preys upon the fears generated by insecurity by offering up what seems to be the only available solution to the problem of personal security. Security takes on the magical form of all commodities but in a way that appears perfectly suited to the phantasmic nature of unseen and unknowable dangers. Echoing Marx's account of commodity fetishism, Neocleous (2008, 153–154) notes:

> Security appears at first sight to be an obvious, even trivial thing... it appears to be nothing other than an object satisfying a human need. But Marx notes of the commodity that 'as soon as it emerges as a commodity, it changes into a thing which transcends sensuousness'. The commodity is thereby given a mystical value arising not from its use-value ... commodities presented in security terms are at an added advantage here, as they appear to serve the satisfaction of a very basic human need. But Marx's point is that commodity-production *per se* is far from obvious and trivial. Tracing the contours of the production of security commodities takes us to the heart of the security industry, a process whereby security becomes fetishistically inscribed in commodified social relations.

Security commodities are *practical* fetishes in the manner discussed in Chapter 1: they both reveal an apparent solution to a problem by concealing its underlying causes. As with all forms of fetishism, the security fetish ascribes to things powers which are social in nature. Commodity fetishism in all of its guises testifies the fundamentally *alienated* conditions of life under contemporary capitalism where both the state and the economy have become alienated from the mass of society. Instead of addressing the root of the problem, we seek security in all the wrong places. As Spitzer (1987, 50) reminds us:

> Instead of bringing us closer together and strengthening the bonds of community and society, the security commodity becomes a means of setting ourselves apart ... Paradoxically, the more we enter into relationships to obtain the security commodity, the more insecure we feel; the more we depend upon the commodity rather than each other to keep safe and confident, the less safe and confident we feel; the more we divide the world into those who are able to enhance our security and those who threaten it, the less we are able to provide it for ourselves.

Note

1   It has been only recently revealed (Medsger 2014) that the documents detailing FBI dirty tricks against political dissidents were stolen in 1971 from an FBI field office by a courageous group of anti-war protesters and subsequently turned over to the mainstream press.

5

Contesting Empire: Beyond the Citizenship Illusion

In one of his final letters to Walter Benjamin in 1940, Theodor Adorno wrote:

> [A]ll reification is a forgetting: objects become purely thing-like the moment they are retained for us without the continued presence of their other aspects: when something of them has been forgotten.
>
> quoted in Bewes (2002)

What has been forgotten? Marx insists that what has been forgotten are the human powers which have been reified in the commodity: the commodity has been spiritualized with the invisible, immaterial substance of value – the expression of human labour in the abstract. Reification, therefore, is not something which has become permanently ossified in the material substrate of the commodity but is rather unstable and subject to alteration. This means that commodity fetishism is *reversible* such that 'reification becomes a volatile concept which may denote mutability as well as fixity, openness as well as closure, remembering as well as forgetting, homogeneity as well as difference' (203). This suggests that the multiple forms of fetishism we have discussed throughout this book are also *reversible*. That is, it should be possible to retrieve the memory not only of those long-forgotten processes of primitive accumulation which ushered in the capitalist commodity form of labour but also of those developed social forms built on its foundation.

Capitalism generates oppositional forms of consciousness immanently, as the exploited and oppressed struggle to improve their circumstances and attenuate the conditions of exploitation (O'Connor 1984, 181).[1] While the use-value of labour means one thing for capital, it may and often does mean something entirely different for labour itself. As Marx (1973, 274) observes in the *Grundrisse*, 'The *use-value* which confronts capital as posited exchange value is *labour*. Capital exchanges itself, or exists in this role, only in connection with *not-capital*, the negation of capital, without which it is not capital the real *not-capital* is *labour*.' In other words, the same processes which produce 'subjects of value' *for* capital also produce struggles which gesture *beyond* capital towards social forms based on alternative value practices (De Angelis 2007, 33). It does so, firstly, because capital is incapable of meeting even the most basic human needs for vast numbers of the world's population owing to its radically unequal distribution of wealth. And secondly, because many refuse complete subjection to capital both in the terms and conditions of the labour process and in the definition of their consumption needs and desires by the commodity form. A central reason for the emergence of such 'counter-subjectivities' lies in the fact that capital does not and cannot produce living labour from within its own operations. As Michael Lebowitz (1992, 48–49) argues, 'Capital as a whole, does not...include within it that which is a "necessary condition for the reproduction of capital" – the maintenance and reproduction of the working class...capital as a whole must posit the wage-labourer outside it in order to exist as such...it is necessary to consider the wage-labourer as she exists outside capital.' This suggests that the rich complexity of human needs, what Marx termed our 'species-being', cannot be fully 'captured' by capital. Wage labour has, in a sense, its own *telos* separate from that of capital; workers are constantly forced into struggle to assert their own needs against the imperatives of capital. Such struggles reach 'all the way down' to questions of discipline and control over the human body both inside and outside the workplace and 'all the way up' to our intellectual and affective needs and desires. The creation of 'subjects of value' depends upon the ongoing *separation* of workers from human needs which cannot be met through capitalist processes. But in so doing, it also generates value subjects and practices of a different kind which challenge the spread of commodity relations, enclosure and dispossession. Working-class people simply have never adhered to the strict separation of economics and politics prescribed by capitalism. They have often pushed at the boundaries of the political sphere, attempting to enlarge and deepen the meaning and range of democratic rights and freedoms. Notions of liberty and equality are always *contested*, not because they are viewed as empty ideological illusions, but because some groups see them as only *partially* adequate vehicles for the realization of their democratic aspirations. To put it another way, in capitalist democracies, different social classes will attempt to pour different social contents into these concepts, to invest them with different meanings.

Crucially, this has included occasional forays into the realm of private property and capitalist accumulation. Historically, subordinate groups have resisted having their labour transformed into wage-labour. Initially, these struggles involved resistance to the imposition of enclosure and the transformation of land and other resources into privately owned commodities. In the early phases of industrialization, craft workers like the much-maligned Luddites fought rear-guard battles against the destruction of customary forms of labour which allowed them a high level of control over the labour process and the imposition of capitalist forms of labour discipline. Later on, workers began to organize themselves collectively in trade unions and political parties of the Left to resist the conditions imposed on them by commodified labour. While playing a central role in fostering the development of capitalism, the state was also forced to mitigate the worsening conditions of industrial labour through laws and legislation which offered some protection against the vagaries of pure market capitalism. Limits on the working day, minimum wage laws, unemployment insurance, pensions, public education and healthcare programmes are all instances where aspects of social life have been wholly or partially de-commodified.[2] While it could be argued that such concessions have allowed capitalism to survive, they are also emblematic of a long history of collective resistance to its depredations and the expansion of domains centred on workers' needs.[3] Organized in political parties and trade unions, the historic Left played a crucial role in expanding social rights and the boundaries of citizenship. For over a century, the organized Left was able to widen and deepen citizenship rights and democratic institutions. As Geoff Eley has observed of European democracy:

> This historic Left had proved more than simply 'good enough'. It doggedly and courageously constructed the foundations of democracy in Europe. It consistently pushed the boundaries of citizenship outward, demanding democratic rights where *ancient regimes* refused them, defending democratic gains against subsequent attack and pressing the case for greater inclusiveness... Between the 1860s and the 1960s... [the historic Left] formed the active center of any broader democratic advance. This is the history of socialism that needs to be recovered and given its due.
>
> Eley (2002, 10)

The collapse or marginalization of the major western Communist parties after 1989, the weakening of trade union struggle as well as changes in the composition of the working class itself have all contributed to the marginalization of the traditional Left in many of the advanced capitalist countries. Such conditions can, of course, lead to despair and fatalism, or worse, the rise of right-wing populist or fascist movements which see their interests as aligned with capitalism domestically and internationally. Elsewhere, however, as seen in parts of Latin America, Southern Europe and the Middle East, there have been explosions of anger and struggle of a more progressive nature. The question remains whether the Left, severely weakened by decades of retreat and defeat under neo-liberalism, can rally the forces necessary to mount a concerted challenge to the rule of capital and the imperial system. David Harvey has suggested that the Left must find new methods of struggle which reflect the changed nature of capitalism in the era of neo-liberalism and imperialism in the form of accumulation through dispossession. The latter has produced struggles which are by nature fragmentary and episodic, often centred on a land dispossession affecting indigenous groups here or the privatization of a service or resource there. The growth of the informal sector and urban slums as a result of land dispossession has led to new demands for urban citizenship based on social redistribution and the control of public space (Prashad 2012, 272). This has led to the need for new and more flexible organizational forms that can quickly respond to such events: 'The whole field of anti-capitalist, anti-imperialist, and anti-globalization struggle has consequently been reconfigured and a very different political dynamic has been set in motion' (Harvey 2003, 174). A similar pattern has been noted in the advanced capitalist states where 'the central force for the fight back has been composed of white-collar workers, potential white-collar students, and public service employees – this pattern has been consistent from the *indignados* to Occupy. Typically urban, these protests target the austerity regime and its social consequences' (Prashad, 251). Harvey's (2003, 176) solution is to call for a link between struggles against the expanded reproduction of capital with those against accumulation through dispossession since they are 'organically linked, dialectically intertwined'. To this list must be added the cross-cutting struggles surrounding race, gender and sexuality, many of which continue to be expressed in terms of demands for greater rights within the ambit of liberal citizenship. But since these forms of oppression often intersect with those of class, there exists the possibility, in the right conditions, of linking them to both anti-capitalist and anti-imperialist struggles.

If Latin America was the first laboratory of neo-liberal empire in the 1970s, it has recently become one of the main laboratories of alternatives to neo-liberalism. While some countries, like Mexico, much of Central America, Columbia, Peru and Chile have remained firmly within the orbit of neo-liberalism and US imperialism, others have pursued a range of progressive, if not explicitly anti-capitalist, directions. While both Brazil and Argentina, under successive centre-Left governments, have introduced some progressive social policies and Keynesian-inspired economic initiatives, they have also strengthened new 'interior bourgeoisies' (Katz 2011, 204) based around finance, industrial exporters, agribusiness and resource extraction, often in cooperation with transnational capital. Ecuador and, to a lesser extent, Bolivia under Evo Morales also remain heavily reliant on mining and fossil fuels which have recently brought them into direct confrontation with the indigenous communities which helped bring them to power. Even in Venezuela, where revolutionary energies have been most sustained, the state remains heavily reliant on oil revenues to fund its many social initiatives. Thus, the 'pink tide' which involved mass insurgencies in Bolivia, Ecuador, Venezuela and Argentina, while central to breaking the ideological grip of neo-liberalism, has yielded more mixed results from the standpoint of any fundamental break with capitalism. As Claudio Katz argues:

> These uprisings reflected the vitality of anti-imperialist, democratic and anti-capitalist traditions, they widely surpassed the normal conventions of social protest, they improved the conditions for securing popular victories, and they have enabled the partial reversal of the series of popular defeats upon which neoliberalism was established. But they did not involve challenges to the capitalist nature of the state, nor develop forms of popular power or military outcomes that characterize social revolutions.
>
> Katz (205)

Even so, the region remains a vital source of discussion, mobilization and experimentation for the international Left. A key area of debate concerns the relationship of popular political forces to governments of the Left. Raul Zibechi has forcefully argued for territorially autonomous zones of resistance, recuperation and capacity-building of the sort found among Zapatista-controlled 'good government' regions in Chiapas in southern Mexico and the Brazilian Landless Movement (MST) which has redistributed thousands of acres of land to landless peasants throughout the country. Such territorial movements have also grown up in urban areas in the *barrios* and *favelas* (shanty towns) which ring most Latin American cities. Urban neighbourhoods under popular control in Caracas, Santiago, Lima, Buenos Aires and La Paz mobilized around issues of housing, water rights and food distribution; and the recuperation of closed factories was pivotal in bringing down traditional governments committed to neo-liberalism and paving the way for the ascendency of Left governments. All such movements are characterized by a number of common characteristics, including a degree of material autonomy often based around subsistence economies oriented towards the production of use-values over exchange-values; the revalorization of cultural identities often most pronounced among indigenous movements including a reassertion of the relationship between work and nature; and a prominent role for women in positions of political leadership.

While autonomous territorial movements have achieved a certain staying power, Zibechi is aware of the dangers facing such movements, not just from the silent stealth of neo-liberalism and hostile governments but also from the seemingly benign activities of NGOs and governments of the Left. International NGOs have tended to sap the energy of social movements by increasing levels of bureaucratization, intensifying links with the state and distancing leaderships from their base, leading to co-optation of the movement: 'Over time, leaders begin to change their profile within the movement, assuming a more technocratic character, specializing in dealing with external funding agencies and procedures in the realm of public administration' (157). Left governments have adopted these new forms of governance, often with a far greater degree of legitimacy than governments of the Right, in an effort to control and pacify movements from below. This new 'capillary state' is 'the most effective agent at disarming the anti-systemic nature of the social movements, operating deep within their territory and as revolt brews' (290). Zibechi is aware of the positive historic significance of the 'pink tide' in shifting the balance of imperial domination in the region and accentuating the crisis of imperialism in the Global North. 'However', he concludes, 'if we look at the issue of emancipation or development, these governments represent a step backward' (324).

For others such as Enrique Dussel (2008), the idea of dispersing power to territorially based movements is premature. While the ultimate goal of revolutionary change should be the dispersion of state power, it should not form the basis of the Left's proximate strategy. Confusing the ideal with the real underestimates the challenges confronting social movements, attempting to push governments further to the Left while maintaining their independence and autonomy. George Ciccariello-Maher (2013, 236) writing about this relationship between popular struggles and the Bolivarian state in Venezuela insists:

> ... we must first strategically accumulate, consolidate, and develop *our own* power if we are ever going to be in a position to 'disperse' the power *of our enemies* later ... this is not a question of putting off the 'real' revolution until later or of accepting institutions 'as is' for the present, but of insisting on the need to understand the accumulation of forces as a revolutionary alternative.

Ciccariello-Maher argues that the Chavista state only became possible against the background of popular insurgency, beginning with the Caracazo rebellion of 1989. These same insurgent movements have continued to challenge 'the very foundations of the state itself, its magic' (238). The dialectic between these two sources of power – popular from below and state power from above – should be understood within the frame of Lenin's concept of dual power:

> Here dual power refers not only to the unstable *situation* of tense equilibrium between this alternative structure and the traditional state but also to the second, nonstate, dual power itself. It is the condensation of popular power from below into a radical pole that stands in antagonistic opposition to the state but functions not as a vehicle to seize the state (unlike Lenin's initial formulation), but instead as a fulcrum to radically transform and deconstruct it... Dual power is, therefore, not a state of affairs but a political *orientation* and the transformative institutions that uphold that orientation, and the question in contemporary Venezuela is whether this orientation will expand or recede.
>
> (240)

Ciccariello-Maher insists that this battle is being fought out daily within the 40,000 communal councils created since 2006 by the Chavez government and within the popular militias and worker-run enterprises. Despite the fact that Chavez himself was radicalized by the popular movements and the hostility of the old Venezuelan ruling class, his actions were not a substitute for struggles from below: 'reaching down from above is simply not the same thing as building it from the bottom up' (250). For the time being, he concludes, 'the popular movements and grassroots revolutionaries have been forced to walk the "tightrope" between the state and the opposition, fighting a war on two fronts against the forces of reaction and against attacks from above on their own autonomy' (254).

The situation in Venezuela may be unique in Latin America, if not the world. In other parts of the continent, Zibechi's calls for autonomy will enjoy wider appeal as a strategy to preserve bases of popular power against powerful enemies both from within and from without. Organizational independence from the state and official party structures has been a hallmark of many recent struggles like the Chilean student movement and the Brazilian Free Fare Movement (MPL) which has been central to the protests surrounding public spending on the World Cup and Olympics. Both of these movements have also had considerable staying power despite the fact that they lack distinct territorial bases to sustain them. Organizational autonomy may insulate these movements for a time against the corrosive effects of the official party system and the state. How they will fair over the longer term as vehicles for building revolutionary capacities and extending the struggle to other sectors such as the organized working class remains an open question. In Southern Europe, the anti-austerity movement has until now confronted governments committed to restoring the power of capital. However, should the Greek Coalition of the Radical Left (Syriza) be elected to power, all of the tensions and complexities of the dual-power strategy advocated by Ciccariello-Maher will likely come into play.

How these debates resolve themselves in practice is dependent on a range of political factors and social forces, including the ability of the imperialist states to disrupt and contain insurgent movements. What does seem more certain is the inability of traditional liberal democracy to satisfy the demands thrown up by the struggles described earlier. As Zibechi notes, enlarging the sphere of liberal citizenship seems to be low on the list of priorities of these movements:

> Their *defacto* exclusion from citizenship seems to have prompted them to build a fundamentally different world. Understanding that the concept of citizenship has meaning only if some are excluded has been a painful lesson learned over the past decades. Hence, the movements tend to press beyond the concept of citizenship, which was useful for two centuries for those who need to contain and divide the dangerous classes.
>
> Zibechi (2012, 16)

While liberal democracy is unlikely to disappear any time soon, it is equally doubtful that the constraints and limits imposed by its basic form are adequate to the challenges which it now confronts. For those in the Global North, the freedoms afforded by liberal capitalism have increasingly become insufficient to address the accelerating wealth inequalities of post-crisis neo-liberalism. Moreover, these populations have been asked to align themselves with an imperial order in which permanent war against unseen enemies has become a fact of life, with few of the material rewards of an earlier phase of empire. In the Global South, accumulation through dispossession in its market and military forms has only worsened pre-existing disparities both within these societies and between the centre and the margins of the global system.

When Marx speaks about the 'illusions about freedom' of bourgeois democracy, he is not suggesting that they are false but rather that their reality masks deeper forms of unfreedom. The 'citizenship illusion' arises from the *reified* structure of capitalist social relations. It is an 'objectified illusion' that reveals and conceals at the same time: it 'reveals' certain limited rights and freedoms within the political sphere while concealing the class inequalities of the economic sphere. As a reified social form, liberal citizenship both constrains certain types of social action while enabling others.[4] As such, it is also tightly bound up with the distribution and exercise of social power: the structural separation of the economic and political spheres was intended to constrain actions which might impinge on the economic powers of capital while enabling purely political rights and obligations. However, this structural division was only ever an imperfect solution to the deeper contradiction between political and legal equality on the one hand and class inequality and exploitation on the other. That is why Marx insists that the political emancipation embodied in abstract citizenship remains only a partial victory. Human emancipation requires the reintegration of political power into society, where work and political life are oriented to fulfilling human needs rather than the demands of profit:

> Only when the real, individual man re-absorbs in himself the abstract citizen, and as an individual human being has become a *species-being* in his everyday life, in his particular work, and his particular situation, only when man has recognized and organized his 'own powers' as *social* powers, and consequently, no longer separates social power from himself in the shape of *political* power, only then will human emancipation be accomplished.
>
> Marx (1844, 21)

Capitalism and imperialism in our own time have intensified the alienation and reification of human needs, which they then seek to satisfy through purely market-based means. If, as Adorno and Benjamin insist, the *reversal* of the fetishistic social forms, which dominate capitalism, must begin with an act of remembrance of what has been forgotten, then we still have some way to go. But as the tenacity of recent struggles has proven, many have not been fooled by either the dream worlds of capital or the 'humanitarian' fantasies of empire. And where memory resides, so also do the seeds of resistance.

Notes

1 As James O'Connor (1984, 181) argues,

> Orthodox Marxism assumes that the value of labor-power is merely its capacity to produce exchange-value; hence it sidesteps the problem of the determination needs, concrete labor, and use-value. However,

it is obvious that real people with real social needs make up society, and their real practice to realize these needs in directly social forms demands some kind of theoretical expression.

2 Rob Albritton (2007, 44) points out, 'Capitalism in the twentieth century ... is no longer simply a progressive commodification of economic life, rather it is a mixture of commodification, decommodification and recommodification with regard to a variety of dimensions that make up the globe.'

3 Commenting on US working-class gains in the 1970s, O'Connor (1984, 186) observes: 'In general, redefinition of needs and reorganization of the social relationships of reproduction functioned as a double critique of US capitalism: first, as critique of wage labor itself second, as a critique of the ways in which the working class construed needs as individual needs satisfiable in the commodity form; in short, as a critique of commodity fetishism.' Rolling back these gains was to become the primary obsession of business and governments from the late 1970s onward.

4 Alex Callinicos (1989), following Anthony Giddens, argues: 'Structures do not simply constrain action. They do not simply act as inert limits, restricting the alternatives open to agents. They are also enabling and are thus present in the actions actually pursued by individuals and groups ... "Power", he (Giddens) says, "is instantiated in action", but agents powers cannot be understood without an analysis of structure' (86).

Bibliography

Abella, Alex. *Soldiers of Reason: The Rand Corporation and the Rise of the American Empire*. New York: Mariner Books, 2009.

Adorno, Theodor W. *Negative Dialectics*. New York: Continuum, 2000.

Albritton, Robert. 'Superseding Lukács: A Contribution to the Theory of Subjectivity'. In *New Dialectics and Political Economy*, edited by Robert Albritton and John Simoulidis, 42–59. New York: Palgrave MacMillan, 2003.

———. *Economics Transformed: Discovering the Brilliance of Marx*. London: Pluto Press, 2007.

Ali, Tariq. *Occupational Hazards*. Interview with Judith Orr. Socialist Review Website. Accessed 17 November 2009. http://www.socialistreview.org.uk/article.php?articlenumber=10936.

———. *The Obama Syndrome: Surrender at Home, War Abroad*. New York: Verso, 2011.

Anees, Saira. 'McLellan: Media During Run-up to Iraq Were "Complicity Enablers."' Accessed 24 August 2013. http//abcnews.go.com.

Arango, Tim and Kraus, Clifford. 'China is Reaping Biggest Benefits of Iraq Oil Boom'. *New York Times*, 2 June 2013.

Arthur, Christopher J. 'The Problem of Use-Value for a Dialectic of Capital'. In *New Dialectics and Political Economy*, edited by Robert Albritton and John Simoulidis, 131–149. New York: Palgrave MacMillan, 2003.

Bacchi, C. L. and Beasley, C. 'Citizen Bodies: Is Embodied Citizenship a Contradiction in Terms'. *Critical Social Policy*, 22 (2): 324–352, 2002.

Bacevich, Andrew J. *American Empire: The Realities and Consequences of U.S. Diplomacy*. Cambridge, MA: Harvard University Press, 2002.

———. *Washington Rules: America's Path to Permanent War*. New York: Metropolitan Books, 2010.

———. 'Avoiding Defeat,' *New York Times*, 10 February 2013.

Ball, Kirstie. 'Workplace Surveillance: An Overview.' *Labor History*, 51(1), 87–106, February 2010.

Banaji, Jairus. *Theory as History: Essays on Modes of Production as Exploitation*. Boston: Brill, 2010.

Bannerji, Himani. *Thinking Through: Essays on Feminism, Marxism and Anti-Racism*. Toronto: Women's Press, 1995.

———. *The Dark Side of the Nation: Essays on Multiculturalism, Nationalism and Gender*. Toronto: Canadian Scholar's Press, 2000.

Barker, Colin. 'A Note on the Theory of Capitalist States'. *Capital and Class*, Spring (2): 118–126, 1978.

Barker, Peter. 'Obama's Turn in Bush's Bind'. *New York Times*, 10 January 2013.

Basso, Pietro and Donis, Giacomo. *Modern Times, Ancient Hours: Working Lives in the Twenty-First Century*. London: Verso, 2003.

Beiner, Ronald. *What's the Matter with Liberalism*. Berkeley: University of California Press, 1995.

Benjamin, Medea. *Drone Warfare: Killing by Remote Control*. New York: OR Books, 2012.

Bergen, Peter L. 'Warrior in Chief'. *New York Times*, 29 January 2012.

Berlant, L. 'National Brands/National Body: *Imitation of Life*'. In *The Phantom Public Sphere*, edited by Robbins Bruce, 173–208. Minneapolis: University of Minnesota Press, 1993.

Bewes, Timothy. *Reification or the Anxiety of Late Capitalism*. London: Verso, 2002.

Blackburn, R. *The Overthrow of Colonial Slavery*. London: Verso, 1988.

Bobbit, Philip. *The Shield of Achilles: War, Peace, and the Course of History*. New York: Alfred A. Knopf, 2003.

Boltanski, Luc and Chiapello, Eve. *The New Spirit of Capitalism*. London: Verso, 2005.

Bonefeld, Werner. 'Money, Equality and Exploitation'. In *Global Capital, National State and the Politics of Money*, edited by W. Bonefeld, and J. Holloway, London: Macmillan, 1995.

Bonefeld, W., Gunn, R. and Psychopedis, K. *Open Marxism*. Volume II. London: Pluto, 1992.

———. *Open Marxism*. Volume III. London: Pluto, 1995.

Boot, Max. *The Savage Wars of Peace: Small Wars and the Rise of American Power*. New York: Basic Books, 2002.

Brenner, Robert. 'What Is, and What Is Not, Imperialism?'. *Historical Materialism*, 14 (4): 79–105, 2006.

Brown University. 'Costs of War Project'. Watson Institute for International Studies. Accessed 17 March 2013. http://costsofwar.org/.

Bukharin, Nikolai. *Imperialism and World Economy – Introduced by V.I. Lenin*. London: The Merlin Press, 1972.

Bush, George. 'Transcript of Radio Address', 2003. Accessed 22 May 2013. http://georgewbush-whitehouse.archives.gov/news/releases/2003/03/20030322.html.

Butler, Judith, Laclau, Ernesto and Žižek, Slavoj. *Contingency, Hegemony, Universality: Contemporary Dialogues on the Left*. London: Verso, 2000.

Callinicos, Alex. *Making History*. Oxford: Polity Press, 1989.

———. *Imperialism and Global Political Economy*. Cambridge, MA: Polity Press, 2009.

Cammack, Paul. 'U.N. Imperialism: Unleashing Entrepreneurship in the Developing World.' In *The New Imperialists: Ideologies of Empire*, edited by Colin Mooers, Oxford: OneWorld Press, 2006.

Ciccariello-Maher, George. *We Created Chavez: A People's History of the Venezuelan Revolution*. Durham, NC: Duke University Press, 2013.

Clarke, S. *The State Debate*. London: MacMillan, 1991.

Cline, William R. 'Public Debt as a Percentage of GDP in Countries Around the World,' *Global Finance*. Accessed 13 August 2013. http://www.gfmag.com/component/content/article/119-economic-data/12370-public-debt-percentage-gdp.html#axzz2yh2iDvdl.

Cockcroft, James D. *Mexico's Revolution Then and Now*. New York: Monthly
   Review Press, 2010.
Cohen, Jean L. 'Changing Paradigms of Citizenship and the Exclusiveness of the
   Demos'. *International Sociology*, 14 (3): 245–268, September 1999.
Crary, Jonathan. *24/7: Terminal Capitalism and the Ends of Sleep*. London: Verso,
   2013.
Das Gupta, T. *Racism and Paid Work*. Toronto: Garamond Press, 1996.
Davis, Mike. *Planet of Slums*. London: Verso, 2007.
Day, Gail. *Dialectical Passions: Negation in Postwar Art Theory*. New York:
   Columbia University Press, 2011.
De Angelis, Massimo. *The Beginning of History: Value Struggles and Global
   Capital*. London: Pluto Press, 2007.
Deinst, Richard. *The Bonds of Debt*. London: Verso, 2011.
de Waal, Alex. 'Dollarized'. *London Review of Books*, 24 June 2010.
Doran, Christopher. *Making the World Safe for Capitalism: How Iraq Threatened
   the US Economic Empire and Had to Be Destroyed*. London: Pluto Press,
   2012.
dos Santos, Paulo. 'On the Content of Banking in Contemporary Capitalism'.
   Historical Materialism, 17 (2): 180–213, June 2009.
Douthat, Ross. 'The Obama Synthesis'. *New York Times*, 13 January 2013.
Duménil, Gérard and Dominique, Lévy. *Capital Resurgent: Roots of the
   Neoliberal Revolution*. Cambridge, MA: Harvard University Press, 2004.
Dussel, Enrique. *Twenty Theses on Politics*. Translated by G. Ciccariello-Maher.
   Durham, NC: Duke University Press, 2008.
Eagleton, Terry. *Ideology*. London: Verso, 1991.
———. *After Theory*. New York: Basic Books, 2003.
Edelman, Peter. 'Poverty in America: Why Can't We End It?' *New York Times*,
   29 July 2012.
Ehrenreich, Barbara and Muhammad, Dedrick. 'The Recession's Racial Divide'.
   New York Times, 13 September 2009.
Eley, Geoff. *Forging Democracy: The History of the Left in Europe, 1850–2000*.
   New York: Oxford University Press, 2002.
Elmer, Greg and Opel, Andy. 'Pre-empting Panoptic Surveillance: Surviving the
   Inevitable War on Terror'. In *Theorizing Surveillance: The Panopticon and
   Beyond*, edited by David Lyon, Cullompton, Devon, UK: Willan Publishing,
   2006.
Eurogroup Statement (21 February 2012) http://www.consilium.europa.eu/
   uedocs/cms_data/docs/pressdata/en/ecofin/128075.pdf.
Ferguson, Niall. *Empire: The Rise and Demise of the British World Order and the
   Lessons for Global Power*. New York: Basic Books, 2004.
Filipovic, Jill. 'America's Private Prison Systmem is a National Disgrace'. *The
   Guardian*. Accessed 28 August 2013. http://theguardian.com/2013/jun/13/
   aclu-lawsuit/.
Fine, Ben. *Social Capital Versus Social Theory*. New York: Routledge, 2001.
——— and Milokanis, Dimitris. '"Useless but True": Economic Crisis and the
   Peculiarities of Economic Science'. *Historical Materialism*, 19 (2): 3–31, 2011.
Fine, Bob. *Democracy and the Rule of Law*. London: Pluto Press, 1986.
Foley, Conor. *The Thin Blue Line: How Humanitarianism Went to War*. New York:
   Verso, 2008.

Fraser, N. 'Rethinking the Public Sphere: A Contribution to the Critique of Actually Existing Democracy'. In *Habermas and the Public Sphere,* edited by Calhoun Craig, 109–142. Cambridge, MA: MIT Press, 1996.

Freeland, Chrystia. 'The Numbers Get Starker for the 99% – and Mitt Romney', *Globe and Mail,* 9 March 2012.

Fukuyama, Francis. *State-Building: Governance and World Order in the 21st Century.* New York: Cornell University Press, 2004.

Gallagher, Brenden. 'Mainstream Media's Biggest 9/11 Fails.' Accessed 21 August 2013. http://www.complexmag.ca/.

Gates, Bill. *The Road Ahead.* New York: Viking Press, 1995.

Globe and Mail. 'US Family Wealth Fell 39% During Crisis,' 12 June 2012.

Global Finance Magazine. 'Public Debt as a Percentage of GDP in Countries around the World'. http://www.gfmag.com/component/content/article/119-economic-data/12370-public-debt-percentage-gdp.htm.

Goldstein, Matthew. '"Bear Stearns" Subprime Path'. *Business Week,* 12 June 2007.

Gowan, Peter. *The Global Gamble: Washington's Faustian Bid for World Dominance.* London: Verso, 1999.

Graeber, David. *Debt: The First 5000 Years.* New York: Melville House Publishing, 2011.

Grandin, Greg. 'Human Rights and Empire's Embrace: A Latin American Counterpoint'. In *Human Rights and Revolutions,* edited by Jeffrey N. Wasserstrom, Greg Grandin, Lynn Hunt and Marilyn B. Young, New York: Rowman and Littlefield, 2007.

———. *Empire's Workshop: Latin America, the United States, and the Rise of New Imperialism.* New York: Metropolitan Books, 2006.

Greenwald, Glenn and MacAskill, E. 'Boundless Informant: the NSA's Secret Tool to Track Global Surveillance Data.' Accessed 6 December 2013. http://www. guardian.co.uk.

Hanieh, Adam. 'Praising Empire: Neoliberalism under Pax Americana'. In *The New Imperialists: Ideologies of Empire,* edited by Colin Mooers, Oxford: OneWorld Press, 2006.

———. 2010. '*Khaleeji*-Capital: Class Formation and Regional Integration in the Middle-East Gulf'. *Historical Materialism,* 18 (2): 35–76.

Harvey, David. *Consciousness and the Urban Experience: Studies in the History and Theory of Capitalist Urbanization.* Baltimore: Johns Hopkins University Press, 1985.

———. *The Limits to Capital.* London: Verso, 1999.

———. *Spaces of Hope.* Berkeley: University of California Press, 2000.

———. *The New Imperialism.* Oxford: Oxford University Press, 2003.

———. 'In What Ways Is the New Imperialism Really New?'. *Historical Materialism,* 15 (3): 57–70, 2007.

———. *A Brief History of Neoliberalism.* Oxford: Oxford University Press, 2007.

———. *The Enigma of Capital: And the Crises of Capitalism.* Oxford: Oxford University Press, 2011.

Hawkes, David. *Ideology.* New York: Routledge, 1996.

Hersh, Seymour M. 'Get Out the Vote: Did Washington Try to Manipulate Iraq's Election?' *The New Yorker,* 18 July 2005.

Holloway, J. *Change the World without Taking Power.* London: Pluto, 2002.

Hyman, Louis. *Debtor Nation: The History of America in Red Ink.* Princeton: Princeton University Press, 2011.

Ignatieff, Michael. *The Lesser Evil: Political Ethics in an Age of Terror.* Princeton: Princeton University Press, 2004.

International Institute for Labour Studies. *World of Work Report 2011: Making Markets Work for Jobs* published 31 October 2011. Accessed 2 July 2013, http://www.ilo.org/wcmsp5/groups/public/---dgreports/---dcomm/---publ/documents/publication/wcms_166021.pdf.

International Labour Organization. Information Sheet No. WT-4. Published June 2004. Accessed 10 July 2013. http://www.ilo.org/wcmsp5/groups/public/---ed_protect/---protrav/---travail/documents/publication/wcms_170717.pdf.

———. *Global Unemployment Rising Again But with Significant Differences across Regions* ilo.org, (22 January 2013).

Jameson, Fredric. *The Cultural Turn.* London: Verso, 1998.

Jappe, Anselm. 'Sohn-Rethel and the Origins of "Real Abstraction": A Critique of Production or a Critique of Circulation', *Historical Materialism*, 21 (1): 2013, pp. 3–14.

Johnson, Richard. 'Reading for the best Marx: History-writing and Historical Abstraction,' pp. 153–201. Johnson, R., McLennan, G.Schwarz, B. and Sutton, D. eds. *Making Histories: Studies in History-Writing and Politics.* London: Hutchinson, in association with the Centre for Contemporary Cultural Studies, University of Birmingham, 1982.

Kagan, Robert. *Of Paradise and Power: America and Europe in the New World Order.* New York: Routledge, 2003.

Kant, Immanuel. *The Critique of Pure Reason.* New York: St. Martin's Press, 1965.

Katz, Claudio. 'The Singularities of Latin America', *Socialist Register 2012.* Toronto: Fernwood Press, 2011.

Kievit, James and Metz, Steven. 'Strategy and the Revolution in Military Affairs: From Theory to Policy'. *Strategic Studies Institute Publication*, June 1995.

Kirby, Holly, et al. 'The Dirty Thirty: Nothing to Celebrate About 30 Years of Corrections Corporation of America'. Accessed 26 August 2013. http://grassrootsleadership.org/cca-dirty-30.

Kirkpatrick, Jeane. 'Dictatorships and Double Standards'. *Commentary*, November 1979.

———. Accessed 20 July 2013. http://www.commentarymagazine.com/article/dictatorships-double-standards/.

Klein, Naomi. *The Shock Doctrine: The Rise of Disaster Capitalism.* Toronto: A.A. Knopf Canada, 2007.

Knafo, Samuel. 'The Fetishizing Subject in Marx's *Capital'. Capital and Class*, 26, Spring 145–175, 2002.

Koring, Paul. 'Almost 44 Million Americans Living Below the Poverty Line'. *Globe and Mail*, 14 September 2011.

Lazzarato, Maurizio. *The Making of the Indebted Man: An Essay on the Neoliberal Condition.* Translated by Joshua David Jordan. Cambridge, MA: MIT Press, 2012.

Lebowitz, Michael. *Beyond Capital.* New York: St. Martin's Press, 1992.

———. *Following Marx: Method, Critique and Crisis*. Chicago: Haymarket Books, 2009.

Locke, John. *The Second Treatise of Government*. Edited by Thomas P. Peardon. Indianapolis: Bobbs-Merrill Co, 1975.

Lukács, Georg. *History and Class Consciousness: Studies in Marxist Dialectics*. Translated by Rodney Livingstone. Cambridge, MA: MIT Press, 1975.

Maass, Peter. 'The Salvadorization of Iraq'. *New York Times*, 1 May 2005.

Mann, James. *Rise of the Vulcans: The History of Bush's War Cabinet*. New York: Penguin Books, 2004.

Marshall, T. H. 'Citizenship and Social Class'. In *Inequality and Society*, edited by Jeff Manza and Michael Sauder, 148–154. New York: W.W. Norton and Co, 2009.

Martin, Randy. *Financialization of Daily Life*. Philadelphia: Temple University Press, 2002.

———. *An Empire of Indifference: American War and the Financial Logic of Risk Management*. Durham: Duke University Press, 2007.

Marx, Karl. 1844. Comments on James Mill, Eléments D'économie Politique. Accessed 10 January 2011. http://www.marxists.org/archive/marx/works/1844/james-mill/index.htm.

———. 1844. *On the Jewish Question*. Accessed 13 November 2006. http://www.marxists.org/archive/marx/1844/jewish-question/index.htm.

———. *Grundrisse*. Harrmondsworth, England: Penguin Books, 1973.

———. *Theories of Surplus Value, Part III*. Moscow: Progress Publishers, 1975.

———. *Capital: A Critique of Political Economy*. Translated by Ben Fowkes. New York: Vintage Books, 1977.

——— and Engels, Friedrich. *The Communist Manifesto*, edited by Joseph Katz. New York: Washington Square Books, 1972.

McClintock, Ann. *Imperial Leather*. London: Routledge, 1995.

McNally, David. *Bodies of Meaning*. Albany: SUNY Press, 2001.

———. 'The Commodity Status of Labour: The Secret of Commodified Life,' In *Not For Sale: Decommodifying Public Life*, edited by Gordon Laxer and Dennis Soron, 39–54. Peterborough, ONo: Broadview Press, 2006.

———. *Global Slump: The Economics and Politics of Crisis and Resistance*. Oakland: PM Press, 2011.

———. *Monsters of the Market: Zombies, Vampires and Global Capitalism*. Chicago: Haymarket Books, 2012.

Medsger, Betty. *The Burglary: The Discovery of J. Edgar Hoover's Secret FBI*. New York: Knopf, 2014.

Miéville, China. *Between Equal Rights: A Marxist Theory of International Law*. Chicago: Haymarket Press, 2006.

Miles, R. and Brown, M. *Racism*. Second Edition. London: Routledge, 2003.

Miles, Robert and Torres, Rodolfo D. 'Does 'Race' Matter? Transatlantic Perspectives on Racism after "Race Relations", in Rodolfo D. Torres, Louis F. Miron and Jonathan Xavier Inda (Eds) *Race, Identity and Citizenship: A Reader*. Oxford: Blackwell Publishers, 2000. pp. 337–354.

Mitchell, Greg. 'Dan Rather Admits Press Failure on Iraq – Hits Corporate Media'. Accessed 21 August 2013. http://huffingtonpost.com/greg-mitchell/.

Montgomery, David. *Citizen Worker: The Experience of Workers in the United States with Democracy and the Free Market during the Nineteenth Century.* Cambridge, MA: Cambridge University Press.

Moody, Kim. *Workers in a Lean World: Unions in the International Economy.* New York: Verso, 1997.

Mooers, Colin. *The Making of Bourgeois Europe: Absolutism, Revolution, and the Rise of Capitalism in England, France and Germany.* New York: Verso, 1991.

———. 'Multiculturalism and the Fetishism of Difference'. *Socialist Studies*, 1 (2): 2006a.

———. ed. *The New Imperialists: Ideologies of Empire.* Oxford: Oneworld Publications, 2006b.

———. 'The New Fetishism: Citizenship and Finance Capital'. *Studies in Political Economy*, 66, 59–84, Autumn 2001.

Moore, Barrington. *Social Origins of Dictatorship and Democracy: Lord and Peasant in the Making of the Modern World.* Boston: Beacon Press, 1966.

Morgenson, Gretchen. 'Secrets of the Bailout, Now Told'. *New York Times*, 12 April 2011.

Murray, Patrick. 'Things Fall Apart: Historical and Systematic Dialectics and the Critique of Political Economy,' In *New Dialectics and Political Economy*, edited by Rob Albritton. and John Simoulidis. New York: Palgrave Macmillan, 2003.

Neocleous, Mark. *Critique of Security.* Edinburgh, Edinburgh University Press, 2008.

Nocera, Joe. 'Risk Management'. *New York Times Magazine*, 4 January 2009.

O'Connor, James. *The Accumulation Crisis.* New York: B. Blackwell, 1984.

Oliver, K. *Family Values.* London: Routledge, 1997.

Ollman, Bertell. 'Market Mystification in Capitalist and Market Socialist Societies'. In *Market Socialism: The Debate Among Socialists*, edited by Bertell Ollman, 81–124. New York: Routledge, 1988.

Oxfam Briefing Paper. *Working for the Few.* 2014. Accessed 2 January 2014. http://oxfam.org.

Pashukanis, Evgeny. *The General Theory of Law and Marxism.* London: Ink Links, 1978.

Patterson, Scott. *The Quants: How a New Breed of Math Whizzes Conquered Wall Street and Nearly Destroyed It.* New York: Crown Business, 2010.

Petras, James and Veltmeyer, Henry. *Empire with Imperialism: The Globalizing Dynamics of Neo-liberal Capitalism.* New York: Zed Books, 2005.

Povoledo, Elizabeth and Carvajal, Doreen. 'Increasingly, Suicide "by Economic Crisis" Is a Symptom of the Downturn in Europe'. *New York Times*, 15 April 2012.

Prashad, Vijay. *The Poorer Nations: A Possible History of the Global South.* London: Verso, 2012.

Putnam, Robert. *Making Democracy Work: Civic Traditions in Modern Italy.* Princeton: Princeton University Press, 1994.

Reguly, Eric. 'Greece: In Six Months a Changed Picture'. *Globe and Mail*, 3 January 2013.

Reich, Robert. 'Only the Rich Are Benefiting from the American Recovery'. *Financial Times*, 2 April 2012.

Retort (Organization: San Francisco, California) and Boal, Iain A. *Afflicted Powers: Capital and Spectacle in a New Age of War*. London: Verso, 2005.

Rieff, David. *At the Point of a Gun: Democratic Dreams and Armed Intervention*. New York: Simon and Schuster, 2005.

Rigakos, George S. *The New Parapolice: Risk Markets and Commodified Social Control*. Toronto: University of Toronto Press, 2002.

Risen, James and Poitras, Laura. 'NSA Examines Social Networkds of US Citizens,' *New York Times*, 29 September 2013.

——— and Lichtblau, Eric. 'How the US Delved Deeper Via Technology,' *New York Times*, 8 June 2013.

Rivera, Amaad, Cotto-Escalera, Brenda, Desai, Anisha, Huezo, Jeannette and Muhamad, Derek. *Foreclosed: State of the Dream, 2008*. Boston: United for a Fair Economy, 2008, www.faireconomy.org.

Robin, Corey. *Fear: The History of a Political Idea*. Oxford: Oxford University Press, 2004.

Roman, Richard and Velasco Arregui, Edur. 'The Fragile Rise of Bourgeois Hegemony and the Neoliberal State in Mexico', *Socialist Studies*, 7: 238–258.

Rosdolsky, Roman. *The Making of Marx's Capital*. London: Pluto Press, 1977.

Rosenburg, Matthew. 'Karzai Says He Was Assured the CIA Would Continue Delivering Bags of Cash'. *New York Times*, 4 May 2013.

Ross, Kristin. 'Ethics and the Rearmament of Imperialism: The French Case'. In *Human Rights and Revolutions*, edited by Jeffrey N. Wasserstrom, Lynn Hunt and Marilyn B. Young, Lanham, MD: Rowman & Littlefield Publishers, 2007.

Saez, Immanuel. 'Income Inequality: Evidence and Policy Implications', Arrow Lecture, Stanford University, January 2013. Available at http://elsa.berkeley.edu/~saez/lecture_saez_arrow.pdf.

San Juan, E. 'Marxism and the Race/Class Problematic: A Re-Articulation'. Accessed 27 October 2003. http://eserver.org/clogic/2003/sanjuan.html.

Saunders, Frances Stoner. *The Cultural Cold War: The CIA and the World of Arts and Letters*. New York: New Press, 1999.

Schwartz, Nelson D. and Dash, Eric. 'Banks Bet Greece Defaults on Debt They Helped Hide'. *New York Times*, 24 February 2010.

Serle, Jack. 'Un Expert Labels CIA Tactic Exposed by Bureau "a war crime" '. *The Bureau of Investigative Journalism*, 21 June 2012.

Seymour, Richard. *The Liberal Defence of Murder*. London: Verso Books, 2012.

Siddiqui, Haroon. 'Legal, Moral and Political Cost of US Drone War'. *Toronto Star*, 30 May 2013.

Simmel, Georg. *The Philosophy of Money*. Translated by Tom Bottomore and David Frisby. London: Routledge, 1990.

Singer, Peter. 'Outsourcing War'. Brookings Institution 2005. Accessed 20 August 2013. http://www.brookings.edu.articles/03/01.

Skinner, Michael. 'Bottom of the 4th Inning of the Great Game: Afghanistan is Now Open for Business'. *The Bullet*, 24 December 2010.

Skocpol, Theda. *States and Social Revolutions*. London and New York: Cambridge University Press, 1979.

Smith, James. Supervisory Duties and the National Compensation Survey. *US Bureau of Labor Statistics*, 2000. Accessed 28 August 2013. http://www.bls.gov/opub/mlr/cwc/supervisory-duties-and-the-national-compensation-survey.pdf.

Smith, Neil. *The Endgame of Globalization.* New York: Routledge, 2005.

Smith, Paul. *Primitive America: The Ideology of Capitalist Democracy.* Minneapolis: University of Minnesota Press, 2007.

Sohn-Rethel, Alfred. *Intellectual and Manual Labour: A Critique of Epistemology.* London: Macmillan, 1978.

Spitzer, Steven. 'Security and Control in Capitalist Societies: The Fetishism of Security and the Secret Thereof', In *Essays in the Sociology of Social Control,* edited by John Lowman et al. 43–58. Aldershot: Gower, 1987.

Stallybrass, Peter. 'Marx's Coat'. In *Border Fetishisms: Material Objects in Unstable Spaces,* edited by Spyer Patricia, 183–207. New York: Routledge, 1998.

Tarrow, Sidney. 'Making Social Science Work across Time and Space: A Critical Reflection on Robert Putnam's "Making Democracy Work"' *American Political Science Review,* 90(2), 389–397, 1996.

Taussig, M. *Mimesis and Alterity: A Particular History of the Senses.* London: Routledge, 1993.

Thatcher, Margaret. 'AIDS, Education and the Year 2000!'. Interview in *Womens' Own.* 23 September 1987. Accessed 27 July 2011. http://www.margaretthatcher.org/speeches/displaydocument.asp?docid=106689.

Thompson, Derek. 'Europe's Record Youth Unemployment: The Scariest Graph in the World Just Got Scarier'. *The Atlantic,* 31 May 2013.

Thompson, E. P. *Whigs and Hunters: The Origin of the Black Act.* London: Penguin, 1977.

Turse, Nick. *The Changing Face of Empire.* Chicago: Haymarket Books, 2012.

U.S. Bureau of Labor Statistics. December 2008. Accessed 11 July 2013. http://www.bls.gov/news.release/archives/empsit_01092009.pdf.

———. News Release, January 2010. Accessed 11 July 2013. http://www.bls.gov/news.release/archives/empsit_02052010.pdf.

US Army. 'Counterinsurgency Manual'. *Headquarters of the Department of the Army,* December 2006.

Walsh, Joan. 'Targeted Killings: OK if Obama Does It?' Accessed 11 June 2013. *Salon.com,* 19 February 2013.

Weizman, Eyal. *The Least of All Possible Evils; Humanitarian Violence from Arendt to Gaza.* London: Verso, 2011.

Wood, Ellen Meiksins. *Democracy against Capitalism: Renewing Historical Materialism.* Cambridge, MA: Cambridge University Press, 1995.

———. *The Origins of Capitalism: The Longer View.* London: Verso, 2002.

———. *Empire of Capital.* London: Verso, 2003.

———. 'Democracy as Ideology of Empire'. In *The New Imperialists: Ideologies of Empire,* edited by Colin Mooers, 9–23. Oxford: Oneworld Publications, 2006.

Yakabuski, Konrad. 'The Pain of Black America Just Got Worse'. *Globe and Mail,* 20 April 2011.

Young, I. M. 'Polity and Group Difference'. In *Feminism and Politics,* edited by Philips Anne, 401–429. Oxford: Oxford University Press, 1998.

Zelizer, Viviana. *The Social Meaning of Money.* New York: Basic Books, 1994.

Zibechi, Raul. *Territories in Resistance.* Translated by Ramor Ryan. Oakland: AK Press, 2012.

Žižek, Slavoj. *The Sublime Object of Ideology.* London: Verso, 1989.
———. 'Class Struggle or Postmodernism, Yes, Please!,' In *Contingency,
Hegemony, Universality: Contemporary Dialogues on the Left,* edited by
Judith Butler, Ernesto Laclau and Slavoj Žižek, 90–135. London: Verso, 2000.
———. 'No Shangrila'. *London Review of Books,* 30: 8, 24, April 2008.
Zolo, Danilo. *Victor's Justice: From Nuremberg to Baghdad.* Translated by
M. W. Weir. London: Verso, 2009.

Index